Praise for *Feel-Good Finance*

"With relatable acuity, *Feel-Good Finance* offers the wisdom and tools to free yourself from the emotional baggage weighing down your money mindset. You can heal yourself and your wallet, all at the same time."

—Heather Boneparth, lawyer, coauthor of
The Millennial Money Fix, and cocreator
of the The Joint Account newsletter

"Whether you're struggling with student debt, budgeting, or saving up for long-term goals, *Feel-Good Finance* will help you tune in to your mental well-being for a life of meaning and authentic connection. Understanding yourself and how you behave with money is necessary to financial wellness. We all deserve financial wellness and Aja walks us through the psychological side to making that happen."

—Tiffany Aliche, *New York Times* bestselling
author of *Get Good with Money*

"*Feel-Good Finance* is a breath of fresh air in a world saturated with finance books that often overlook the true drivers of our financial behaviors. As the cofounder of Trauma of Money, I see the crucial need for Aja's approach, which goes beyond mere financial literacy to address the deep-seated psychosocial factors influencing our relationship with money. This book is an essential tool for anyone looking to heal their financial wounds as a result of collective, generational, or relational trauma and scarcity and reclaim generational wealth."

—Chantel Chapman, CEO and cofounder of Trauma of Money

"*Feel-Good Finance* takes us on a journey we all need to understand and heal our relationship with money. With empathy and heart, Aja guides us through understanding the root of our money beliefs and empowers us with the tools to align our money with our values."

—Farnoosh Torabi, author of *A Healthy State of Panic*

"Aja Evans takes readers on a journey through money's deeper levels of meaning with warmth, wisdom, and wit. In *Feel-Good Finance*, she offers a practical guide to learning to heal and grow *yourself*, not just your bank account balance."

—Amanda Clayman, financial therapist

Feel-Good Finance

Untangle Your Relationship
with Money for Better
Mental, Emotional, and
Financial Well-Being

Aja Evans

BenBella Books, Inc.
Dallas, TX

Feel-Good Finance copyright © 2024 by Aja Evans

"Money" icon on page 96 and throughout is by Adrien Coquet from thenounproject.com
"Tissues" icon on page 24 and throughout is by Cédric Stéphane Touati from thenounproject.com

BenBella Books, Inc.
10440 N. Central Expressway
Suite 800
Dallas, TX 75231
benbellabooks.com
Send feedback to feedback@benbellabooks.com

BenBella is a federally registered trademark.

Printed in the United States of America
10 9 8 7 6 5 4 3 2 1

Library of Congress Control Number: 2024024290
ISBN 9781637745434 (trade paperback)
ISBN 9781637745441 (electronic)

Editing by Lyric Dodson
Copyediting by Jessica Easto
Proofreading by Rebecca Maines and Cheryl Beacham
Text design and composition by Aaron Edmiston
Cover design by Sarah Avinger
Cover image © Sarah Avinger (tissue box and money) and iStock / Prostock-Studio (hand)
Printed by Lake Book Manufacturing

This book is dedicated to baby Aja and to anyone who has ever felt bad about themselves because of money. You are not alone.

Contents

Contents

Chapter 1

Where Shall We Begin?

It's a night to remember as you're out for a celebratory dinner with friends. The wine is flowing freely, and the shared dishes keep coming. As laughs and conversations die down, the check arrives at the center of the table. The energy shifts almost immediately. You'd barely notice it but for the slight pause in the conversation. Someone's hand reaches, kicking off the chain reaction of everyone making a show of bringing out their wallets and purses. You've just landed smack-dab in the middle of the ultimate question for a night out: Who foots the bill? Or at least what portion?

So many of us have done this dance, navigating how to pay the bill at a group event—whether it is a birthday dinner, bachelorette party, or reunion group meal. We often find ourselves stuck in our feels, downing our last mimosa and wondering how the ten-person bill is going to be handled. Not having the conversation about the pending bill beforehand can lead to some dicey situations, but those discussions must be had. Across the internet, these conversations are less uncomfortable, perhaps due to the anonymity the web provides. Whether on podcasts or online forums, folks often ask the tough questions: Does the host of the party pay? Should the person being celebrated contribute to the bill? Does each family pay for themselves or split the entire bill for everyone? Were the attendees all aware of the price of the restaurant before going? What happens if you don't drink? The list of scenarios is endless.

When I first moved to New York City in 2014, I was offered a job that paid $60,000. To be honest, before I actually started living in the city and collecting my paycheck, I thought I would not only feel rich, but I would *be* rich. (Our ideas about high income rarely end up panning out the way we envision them.) In 2014, the US Census Bureau reported that the median individual American salary was $53,657.[1] So, in the grand scheme of things, $60,000 was a lot of money for a single person without many responsibilities—more than the combined income of some households. I would have plenty of money, I thought.

I spent accordingly, going out for happy hour with friends, making it rain at brunches, shopping, and traipsing around New York as if I did not have to worry about anything. I was wrong; I most definitely needed to be worrying about money. At the time, I kept my car and the note that went with it. I was, and still am, paying off my student loans. I was commuting once a month via car to Boston to maintain a relationship with my now husband, and on top of all of that, I was attempting to maintain a lifestyle that, frankly, I could not afford.

I wouldn't have been able to articulate it at the time, but it felt important to keep up with my peers; if I couldn't afford something (that I deemed reasonable), it felt like some deep insult to my sense of self. When I went out with my friends, who frequently had larger salaries than mine, I felt like I needed to blend in, look the part, and belong. At the time, this meant throwing down my card at the group dinner, agreeing to split the check, and ignoring my urge to tally what everyone got and compare. As much as I wanted to bring it up, something stopped me. I wasn't yet brave enough to push against the barrier inside of myself. I also wasn't ready to admit to myself that these consistent actions would ruin my mood *and* my financial well-being. Don't get me wrong, I was having a blast, but I was swiping on hope and a prayer, trying to check my balance on my BlackBerry under the table and moving money to escape overdrafting.

And I purposely hadn't even gotten a cocktail like everyone else. I only got water.

Our Money Stories

The narratives we develop around our money are based on a variety of factors, including our lived experiences, the experiences of our family members, and even intergenerational and historical trauma. Financial literacy and money management aren't often skills we are all explicitly taught in adolescence, and while personal finance gurus have told us it's "all about education," my experience says that it is most certainly not just about the numbers. While financial education is important, how you understand yourself and how you interact with money will always play a role in what you do with it and how you ultimately feel about it. The vast majority of us are financially struggling not only because of what we do with our money but because of how our feelings impact our behaviors and, therefore, our wallets and bank accounts.

Like many of my peers, in my twenties, I felt like I should be more ready, more prepared, or more on top of things. The fact that I had entered adulthood, scored a "big girl job," moved into an apartment, and was becoming more self-reliant made me feel like I should know exactly what to do. The messages I internalized from a young age told me I was an adult at eighteen. So, as a newly minted "adult," being thrust into the "real world" armed with my degrees, I was supposed to have some amorphous internal guide directing me toward all my wildest dreams. Unfortunately, adjusting to that level of responsibility takes time, even if the major responsibility is for yourself. This feeling increased tenfold when I became a parent. To be honest, the level of confidence, maturity, and direction I feel at thirty-seven is what I anticipated feeling in my midtwenties.

In talking to people, both personally and professionally, I have learned that at some point we have all felt like we should be looking to someone more senior to be in charge when, in fact, that someone is you. It is interesting how our child mind views wealth compared to reality, a reality that's further complicated once we start learning about taxes, interest rates, and debt-to-income ratios. For many, no matter their age, the display of cars, clothes, vacations, and homes feels like insight into how much money someone has, but what I started to understand in my midtwenties during my financial awakening was that being rich and being wealthy were two very different things. Being *rich* to me is more about wealth signifiers, the aforementioned material items and luxury goods that signify someone has discretionary money to spend. Being *wealthy* is more about the money you don't see—high net worth, valuable assets, and smart investments. It's the money that isn't liquid or easily spent, that can be passed on for generations. There are plenty of people who are extremely wealthy but don't "look" rich. And this is where people get caught up. Instead of having conversations about the nuanced nature of actual wealth, finances, and our own experiences with money, we put these discussions off for another day that conveniently never comes and focus our attention on material items we've gained or hope to attain. And this lack of in-depth money conversations is likely the culprit behind our ill feelings toward money as a collective.

Here's the truth: Talking about money is hard. People have a variety of unspoken rules and expectations about how to handle all types of money situations, often rooted in their own personal narratives and history with money. And we so rarely talk about it. But that ends here. Oh yes, friend, we are going to talk about money and—shocker—I want you to dive into understanding your relationship with money and really swim around in it. Why? Because we need to be able to talk about money to change how we think about it and disentangle from all our unhealthy money mindsets and narratives.

Think of this book as your financial awakening and the tool kit to begin addressing what you uncover in the process. The information we'll cover here will help you change how you think about and behave around money so you can live your best life, whatever that may look like for you. Instead of feeling uncomfortable, confused, or unsure about your finances, you will have the tools to explore the origins of your relationship with money, understand how your current money mindset came to be, and choose the financial behaviors that work best for you so you can feel confident in your money moves now and in the future. By the end of this book, you will be able to effectively save, spend, and invest, all while enjoying your life without fear of stepping on an emotional land mine of past money baggage that leaves you harming your financial health.

A Financial Awakening

My financial awakening began during the Easter holiday in 2015. I made the drive from Astoria, New York, to my aunt's house in Crown Heights for dinner. Among the kids running around, pots clanking, and gospel music playing in the background, I had an opportunity to catch up with my cousin, Man (Tim to people outside of the family), who's a few years older than me, married, and well into growing his family. I, a single woman with no children, had the audacity to complain to him about feeling stressed, mainly financially stressed. (Looking back now, the "problems" I had then make me giggle. Not that twenty-somethings don't have problems; they do, but the irony isn't lost on me about the difference in issues given our ages and level of responsibility. Shout-out to Man for being patient with me and my blind spots.)

As we caught up, he casually mentioned that I might want to learn more about personal finance; at the time I knew nothing. He shared, "It can be hard when you're on your own, but learning about money and paying more attention to it could really help you harness that financial power." He didn't know it, but that small conversation changed the trajectory of my life and shifted my perspective just enough for me to try something new. I went home and began consuming whatever content I could find about debt, investing, and money management. He and I now joke about how our families are probably completely burnt out on how much we can sit and talk about money. What can I say? The family finances are better for it.

It did not take long for my love of personal finance to start bleeding into my work as a therapist. I found myself inviting the conversation about money and the feelings it brought up into sessions with my clients. What were they struggling with? How were they feeling about their money? Were they feeling as bad as I had felt before I got my money in check? Spoiler: They were, and I needed to help. The more I talked about it, the more I realized how much people were suffering. And here was one of the more fascinating parts: It wasn't only about what they did or didn't have but also what they started to tell themselves as a result.

As I did the work of diving into myself and realizing how deeply my mindset and behavioral patterns impacted my life, I continued to make connections about how our psychology influences how we behave with money. The snippets of traditional financial advice I had internalized in the past—"money isn't emotional; put your feelings aside and just look at the numbers," "focusing on saving is the best thing you can do for yourself," and "women should not worry about money," to name a few—had wronged me and countless others. You can try to separate money and emotions all you want, but it's kind of bullshit. Anything a human does, touches, or thinks about has the potential to be emotional. To separate the two is to ask us to ignore parts of our instincts, to deny our human nature. I saw the connections so clearly in my personal and professional practices, so why did it still feel so strange to talk about? Why weren't we talking about the very thing we all have to navigate in some way, shape, or form? Why weren't we having open and honest conversations about money with our loved ones, partners, family, friends, or colleagues? What was stopping us?

What I found through my work was that our collective fear, shame, and vulnerability was stopping us dead in our tracks from being more open. We're taught, in so many words, that money is taboo, a secret to discuss only with those closest to you, if that. And in the Black community, that better only include family . . . and not just any family—strictly the adults around you. But it goes even deeper than family taboos.

I saw a post on LinkedIn a while back that went into detail about the seven reasons why people are poor. Of the seven reasons, only one scratched the surface on the gross injustices surrounding a "lack of access to jobs and resources" that occur in this country. Instead, this writer chose to quickly skate over the systemic inequalities and inequities that exist in the United States for anyone who's not a white male. As I continued to read, I felt my body getting warm with anger. When I was at my brokest, I quickly realized how expensive it was to simply exist without spending astronomical amounts of money. The looks I have gotten when I share what my upbringing looked like versus the expectation of what *every* Black woman's experience must have been like, sadly, no longer shocked me. We are not a monolith! Life was good, but it was most definitely not without struggle. It's quite ignorant to ignore what so many of us have had to go through—systematic racism, discrimination in the workplace, microaggressions and backhanded compliments, and lack of relatable mentorship, to name a few—while continuing to show up to work, live, exist, and attempt to thrive just like everyone else.

All of this plays a part in informing our mindset and relationship with our finances, and as you can see, for the most part, this foundation was laid for us without our consent. That is why I wrote this book. I cannot and will not, for another second, sit and listen to the rationalization of wealth inequality being reduced to mere mindset, a lack of emergency funds, and spending above your means. Yes, those things matter and can have massive impacts on your ability to grow wealth, but they do not exist in a silo. The financial circumstances many people find themselves in today are also cultivated by a need for survival, denial of access, limited opportunity, and the necessity to cope with a system that was not built for everyone to thrive.

Rewriting Your Money Story

Understanding how the financial system, human psychology, and personal experience combine to shape your money mindset and money narrative will ultimately impact how you behave with your money and how you feel about it. Your **money mindset** is the lens in which you think, perceive, view, and understand money, while your **money narrative**, or **money story** (I will use these interchangeably), is the culmination of all your lived experience with regard to what you have observed and learned about money. It includes the financial experiences of you and those around you. In a nutshell, your money story is how you make meaning about money through what you have experienced. Any intel you receive about money and finances adds to your money story.

Understanding your money mindset and money narrative is a critical part of your financial journey. Although financial education is important, it is only one piece of the puzzle. Financial education needs to be coupled with understanding yourself and your background. It helps to understand that, even when you have the best laid plan for your finances and are working the plan, life can and will often get in the way. Not only life, but you (yep, I said it) will often get in your own way, and most of the time it will be without your even knowing it.

There's a lot to unpack here, so think of this book as your personal financial therapy session with me. Throughout these pages, we will explore your personal history and feelings about money with the goal of raising your awareness and, therefore, helping you be more intentional about your money moves. This book is for you if . . .

- you continue to feel bad about past money mistakes.
- no matter how hard you try, you feel like you won't ever get to the place you want to be financially.

- budgeting, underspending, or overspending have made you feel uncomfortable or bad about yourself.
- you feel like you will never get it right and don't know why.

I can promise you, you are not alone. Together, we are going to approach your relationship with money from a different angle, the emotional one, connecting what you may be feeling when you make money moves to how it impacts your mental health.

First, we will walk through the teachings and experiences that contribute to your money mindset through historical, personal, and psychological contexts. We'll explore the messages about money your family and ancestors may have been exposed to, which contributed to their behaviors and perceived financial capabilities. We'll delve into some of our most innate desires and needs as humans, focusing specifically on the impulse to feel connected and the impact this can have in the financial realm. We'll shine a light on why you do the things you do with money or, in most cases, *don't* do the things you think you "should." Then, we'll explore the process of understanding where the messages, narratives, and beliefs around money developed and how the culmination of your life experiences created your current money mindset.

Next, we'll address five common limiting beliefs I work through with myself and my clients and how they impact what you do with your money. The anxiety that arises from an expensive group dinner is but one example of how our money stories impact our lives. From hoarding your money for a rainy day to spending it all to keep up with the Joneses, we'll cover a range of money mindsets that may be holding you back. Throughout each chapter, I will offer financial guidance to help inform what you can do to start changing your finances and mindset for the better.

And finally, we'll wrap everything up with your very own step-by-step guide to true financial wellness, including:

- Getting financially naked
- Defining your money goals
- How to handle debt
- The importance of different bank accounts
- Creating a money plan
- And much more . . .

So, get comfortable, get some water, and maybe get some tissues. We are about to embark on a journey to financial wellness that will help explain why your relationship with money is the way it is and where those feelings and behaviors may be coming from. Now, let's get down to business as we begin with this question: Why do so many of us feel like we are bad with money?

Chapter 2

Historical and Personal Context

Like many things in life, but particularly in therapy, reflect-ing on the past allows us to better understand both the present and future. I take a psychodynamic approach in my practice, which focuses on the psychological roots of emotional suffering and is centered around self-reflection and exploring problematic patterns and relationships in the client's life.[2] It took me a long time to truly embrace it, but now that I have, I can't unsee its value. In everyday terms, the psychodynamic approach allows my client and me to dive into their histories to figure out where their beliefs started and how they have been integrated into their current thoughts, behaviors, relationships, and life overall. In understanding how they have lived and reacted in the past, I am able to recognize patterns that may or may not be showing up in unhealthy ways. I frequently incorporate other approaches, like cognitive behavioral therapy (CBT), which focuses on the person as a whole, into my practice, but I find, particularly when I am diving into money, that going back to the past is a must, and I always do my best to make it fun. We can find ways to laugh through parts of the pain.

Our relationship with money is no different from other patterns, habits, and behaviors we display within other parts of our lives. Our ways of being most frequently develop in response to our life experiences, so it is only fair that we first examine our personal history within a broader historical context, both individually and systemically, as it informs where we are today.

Let's level with the current money landscape and be honest in saying that the racial wealth gap is atrocious. White families hold ten times the amount of wealth that their Black and Latinx counterparts do.[3] Liz Mineo, a staff writer for the *Harvard Gazette*, stated in her piece, "Racial Wealth Gap May Be the Key to Other Inequities," that the racial wealth gap "represents, scholars say, the accumulated effects of four centuries of institutional and systemic racism and bears major responsibility for disparities in income, health, education, and opportunity that continue to this day."[4] Sadly, the gender wealth gap provides similar numbers, with the average American woman earning about $0.82 for every dollar a man makes.[5] While the statistics for Black, Indigenous, and people of color (BIPOC) are worse than the gender wealth gap, none of this will do! We know that the racial wealth gaps are horrendous and continue to get worse as other marginalized identities are considered.

In spite of these life-altering inequalities, and a whole host of other implications, we have been fed a narrative that money isn't emotional. You already know I completely disagree. How much our identities impact who we are, the amount of money we can make in society, and what we do with that money cannot be separated from the nuances of finances in general. And all of this naturally leads to big, valid feelings. So much comes up for my clients when we start getting into the weeds of their finances, and I imagine the same will happen with you. So I urge you to give yourself an opportunity to feel. Give yourself the space, alone time, and grace to allow whatever emotions may come up to just be. Don't try to rationalize yourself out of the thought or feeling. Instead, allow it to be there. Be present with the emotion—feel it. If you need to cry, cry. If you are angry, be angry. Allow yourself to sit with the feeling and let it move through you. This is often a challenging part of the process for my clients, and in particular Black women, because so often we've been told, verbally or otherwise, to not show emotion, and when we do, it is taken for weakness. Many of us have not been afforded the luxury of displaying our vulnerability enough. I want to make it clear that our relationship with money is about more than just the numbers, and our very valid reactions to the numbers—our feelings about money—develop in direct response to our life experiences.

In this chapter, we will dive right in to get to the root of where these feelings come from. We'll begin to uncover the origins of your money story and identify the impact it has on your money mindset. We'll look at how your collective trauma, family life, upbringing, and lived experiences combine to form your money story and how this story solidifies to become your money mindset. The narratives we hear over and over often become our beliefs. I'll also provide an example of how all these components alchemize through my own personal money story, including my upbringing in downtown Albany, my yearning for Abercrombie & Fitch, and the beginnings of my financial awakening.

But before we can begin examining our personal contexts, we need to take a closer look at our shared historical context. After all, history influences how we conceptualize the world around us. So in the wise words of BLACKstreet, "What we gonna do right here is go back, way back. Back in time."

A Brief History Lesson

Strap in, friends, things are about to get heavy for a minute. As we know, the history of Black people in the United States is obviously fraught with tension, violence, pain, and suffering.

But despite all the pain, there have also been bright spots. Our history is filled with cultural wins like Madam C. J. Walker becoming the first self-made Black millionaire, the election of Barack Obama, the gifts of Beyoncé, Oprah, and Rihanna, and Robert Smith wiping out the debt of the 2019 Morehouse graduating class. (Be like him and grow your wealth to help the community, but be better and make sure you pay your taxes.) Even with these triumphs, including the growth of Black wealth and so many other amazing advances, we have to be honest about where it started and how far we still have to go.

The lasting impact of slavery is continuously felt in how Black people are treated and viewed to this day, especially in the context of its economic impact. Dissecting the landscape in which we have been attempting to build financial stability is an eye-opening exercise. The level of wealth created from the slave trade and its supporting industries is astronomical—truly mind-blowing. Slavery literally turned the United States into a successful capitalist country. The output in cotton production nearly doubled between 1790 and 1859, creating a billion-dollar global industry. To put that into perspective, that would be equivalent to around $39 billion today. The results were so monumental, in fact, that the industry of slavery (which feels painful to say) was the United States' *biggest* industry, bigger than banks, railroads, and factories combined.[6]

Throughout time, we have constantly battled our collective history and its impacts on our ability to build wealth. As much as I want to dive into specific examples of how Black wealth has been stifled, crushed, or stolen, it is hard to reduce the magnitude of centuries of history to a few short paragraphs. Instead, I want to focus our time together on dissecting how the historical context of our lives influences and affects how we think, feel, and behave with our money. To do that, we have to explore not only our minds but also our bodies. Why? Because the body keeps score.

What does that mean? Well, our trauma can be coded into our DNA and "saved" in the body. How? While there is a lot of research still to be done, especially focused on people of color (I am looking at you, academia and those that fund such research), researchers have learned that if a parent experiences high stress and/or traumatic events during pregnancy, the potential for the baby to experience depression, PTSD, and suicidality go up. In fancy academic terms, "transgenerational epigenetic transmission is defined as the transmission of genomic information from one generation to the next without changing the main structure of DNA."[7] That is right, folks—stress and trauma can literally be passed down genetically through generations, with each cell encoded with the trauma of our ancestors. This has nothing to do with lived experience or information learned growing up; the change in DNA is simply the starting point of life.

This is extremely important to keep in mind when we think about how Black people are treated under this country's systems. We shall not be fooled by the global phenomenon that is

Hamilton; there was no room for the opinions of Black people, people of color, or women when the US financial system was created, though Lin-Manuel Miranda's version is most definitely a version of truth I would prefer. Looking at the financial and emotional implications of the origin story of Black people in the United States is a part of *all* our money stories, no matter your racial or ethnic background. I know this is a hard realization, but being aware of the potential privilege and influence of the past on our present lives is absolutely necessary.

And remember, what we may be calling "history" is not relegated to the distant past. I was shocked to learn that all women were denied access to open a bank account without connection to a man until the 1960s. Friends, that was not long ago! My mom was born in the late 1950s, positioning her to be a middle schooler when she got her first bank account. When I was told this nugget of information, I of course had some questions. Did she know she was making history walking into the bank with my grandmother? How did she feel? What was her experience like? Shit, were people staring? My mother had no idea she was part of the first generation to have a bank account without being tied to a man. Not to mention being a little Black girl prancing into the bank to open an account in the '60s. She said she felt nothing but pride walking into the bank with her brothers and my grandmother to open her account. That is fucking beautiful.

The shift in thought over time has been immense. It is only with decades of effort, advocacy, shifting, learning, and growing that enough change has taken place to get us where we are today. Understanding that people are complex and hold various ways of identifying continues to be a place of growth for us. Intersectionality, the connection of how holding multiple identities combines to create patterns of oppression, will always be in play when we talk about money. As much as we may want or try to avoid it, identity will always influence how we are seen and how we see others, which can have ripple effects on all areas of life.

From the Collective to the Interpersonal

Why does all this matter? History influences how and what we learn, ultimately adding to how we conceptualize the world around us. Your views are informed by everything you take in from people, media, overheard conversations, and images; all information is information, no matter how big or small. This, once again, is no different with money. Can you imagine the messages your family could've passed down about money throughout the generations if they were given the space and opportunity to visibly heal, emotionally and financially, from the civil rights movement and before? This is how our money mindsets and money stories begin. Every bit of information you received from other people when you were young—feeling tension in the house as payday grew closer, feeling pressured to perform at school to meet the demands of your parents, or even assuming that, as a woman, you could not or did not need to make money—informed how you think and behave around money today. This applies not only to how it works but how you work with it.

Tiny humans are sponges that take in everything. Nothing gets erased or filtered out simply because it isn't the best information. Everything you experience goes into formulating your money mindset and, eventually, your money story. Watching how others (our parents, for a lot of us) earned, spent, saved, and talked about money laid the foundation for how you would interact with it. Children start to grasp the concept of money around three years old. I remember watching my daughter at this stage, and—yikes!—it was a time for my partner and me to be really mindful of how we spoke about and behaved around money so we could pass down healthier money relationships. The groundbreaking study "Habit Formation and Learning in Young Children" found that our money foundation is solidified between ages seven and nine.[8] It's interesting to think that we're years into building a foundation for our understanding of money at a point in our lives when we aren't even old enough to make any. From inflection and body language to watching how money is used to cope, your personal experiences around the adults in your life—good, bad, and the ugly—are all lessons for you to learn from.

A Moment for Reflection

These boxes will represent where I am hoping you will take a pause to reflect, lament, or examine your own experience and how what you have read shows up in your life.

Before we move on, I invite you to start thinking about your own family dynamics and relationship with money. You may be surprised how quickly you start to make connections and fill in the blanks for your own story. In a journal, answer the following questions: What was your first money memory? What details of your life have informed your money beliefs? What memories start coming to mind? No need to dissect them yet, we will get there. For now, just allow them to come into view and acknowledge their importance. No feeling is too small.

The Formation of Money Habits

I have a client we'll call Mellody, who I worked with in conjunction with their partner for couple's therapy. Mellody had recently shared a story about going to see their grandmother. While visiting, Mellody's grandmother disclosed that when she moved north from Mississippi to escape her abusive marriage, she had to hide the fact that she was a single mother and was forced to have her brother purchase her home under his name because women did not have access to credit for a mortgage until 1974. This bomb-ass lady moved across the country, hid the fact that she was a single mother, got her brother to purchase a home with *her* money, and raised her two children by herself while pretending she was married because of the optics of being a single Black mother. Phew!

One of those two children was Mellody's mother, who as a little girl had been watching and witnessing all her mother lived through. Among many lessons lived and learned, the importance of stretching a dollar was highlighted. It was clear in our sessions that Mellody's mother had integrated those lessons into her own parenting style. There was no "McDonald's money," and no extra was reserved for special occasions. Mellody's mother taught her children to relentlessly rely on themselves and save their money, and that there was only one way they would be able to provide for themselves one day: completely alone.

How, you might wonder, would this show up in Mellody's money habits? Glad you asked. Mellody and their spouse came to see me because of Mellody's struggle to rely on anyone else. Ordinarily, this might not be seen as an issue, but preparing for marriage and not being able to feel like you can rely on your spouse (whether you need to or not) can cause strife. Mellody believed they had to be able to provide for their spouse, but never the other way around. This can be tricky, as life comes with unexpected moments of fluctuating salaries, unemployment, and other circumstances. Mellody not only wanted to have money saved up as a couple but also believed they needed an exorbitant amount of money saved in an individual savings account "just in case." Now, let me be clear. I do not mind that Mellody wanted their own money saved separately. In fact, I often encourage this (more on this later). However, what we were working on was how Mellody's money narrative had negatively affected their relationship.

In short, Mellody ended up losing their job, and their money mindset of self-reliance above all else became a crushing burden. They struggled to feel as if they were "pulling their weight" in the relationship because they were making less than their partner. Mellody was cutting spending left, right, and center to lessen their financial needs. Their partner was happy to compensate financially for the shift in income, but Mellody resisted. Mellody had a hard time accepting that their inability to contribute equally to the family did not mean they were a burden. Sometimes the narratives we develop as children keep us safe, but as we age and our life circumstances change, those same narratives need to evolve so they don't hold us back. Mellody and I are still working together to rewrite the narrative that had once served them and their family so much. I place no fault on Mellody's mother or grandmother, but the way they lived with money (again, through no fault of their own) most certainly influenced how Mellody saw their ability to contribute to the world and their relationship.

So many of us have experienced this and continue to live in past methodologies that no longer serve what our lives look like today. The influence systems have on our lives can be lasting, even though we live in different times. We witness the behaviors of those around us in response to what they lived through and were taught, and those ideas can last through generations, as do the systems, if they're not acknowledged, challenged, and changed.

Financial Trauma

Reshma Saujani, founder of Girls Who Code and Moms First, was a guest on *The Diary of a CEO*, a podcast that highlights the inner workings and lives of high-performing CEOs. When speaking about her upbringing, Reshma shared how hard her family worked to make ends meet and how difficult it was to give anyone resources for excess when there wasn't enough. This sentiment is one I have heard from many of my clients who grew up not having a lot and now live with a scarcity mentality surrounding money, no matter their current financial situation. It has shifted how they think about risk, saving, spending, and whether they feel able to explore their passions. When there are no resources, potentially "wasting" them to follow your passion feels like a luxury. Survival is of the utmost importance, passion is secondary, and this impacts how people approach work, security, and life. Certain professions (you know, the ones your family often push on you) may provide security; however, the desire for security can backfire when people realize they hate their jobs and potentially feel the same way about their lives overall. They end up feeling like they can't shift, change, or escape because of a fear of financial instability, even if that means they're stuck in an entry-level position making less money.

The story of economic hardship is one that so many of us have lived. Financial trauma, a stressful financial event or crisis that impacts you emotionally and psychologically, is extremely common. People who have experienced financial struggles or scarcity may have dealt with a myriad of financially traumatic experiences, like food and housing insecurity, bankruptcies, loss of employment, the realization that your parents trashed your credit when you were a child, the psychological discomfort of feeling less than due to not being able to make ends meet—the list is endless. That shit is stressful.

Kate Sortino, a freelance journalist, perfectly described what childhood poverty did to her mindset in her piece "How Growing Up Low Income Messed Me Up as an Adult and How I Overcame It" for the Financial Diet.[9] She wrote, "Growing up, my mom and I were unglamorously poor. *Periodically living in our van* poor. 'Will we eat dinner tonight or just pretend we did?' poor." Kate goes on to share how profoundly unprepared she was to enter adulthood and ended up taking on an astronomical amount of student loan debt to pay for school and take care of herself: Two months after turning eighteen, she had over $100,000 of future debt. "I'm not looking to assign blame, but it's hard to talk about childhood poverty without discussing exactly how completely effed so many of us start our lives," Kate said of her experience.

When lamenting the advice she received from her upbringing, she noted how hard it was not to buy into a poverty mindset when that's the reality of everyday life:

The interest grows faster than the money can be made, and being poor is terribly expensive. The poverty mindset ingrained in me was powerful. I became a hoarder and compulsive shopper. I had disordered eating. My anxiety was constant . . . When you don't know when your next meal will come, you want to eat as fast as possible before it's taken away. That's what poverty is like. You have very little, and it seems like everyone wants what little tiny bit you have. It's exhausting and infuriating, and it feels like you're being suffocated. You work hard just to have nothing to show for it. Poverty and debt are treated like personal failures, and the shame of it is constant . . . I didn't even want to play by the rules because the rules felt very unfairly stacked against me.

Eventually, Kate decided she needed to make some drastic changes to right her financial life. She no longer wanted to feel stuck in her poverty mindset. "No amount of being sad or mad about that fact would change it," she wrote. "I had to write my narrative: My financially disadvantaged upbringing was not my *fault*, but my future was my *responsibility*. So, I educated myself."

After that moment, Kate went on to work her ass off, sell stuff, and eventually pay off her debt. Although debt-free, the influence of her life experience, the teachings from her mom, and the process of digging out from the poverty mindset will be lasting.

It Always Comes Back to the Patriarchy

Who you are is made up of a variety of factors, including your genetics, psychology, and the meaning you put on your life experiences. Though you and another person (such as a sibling) may have been raised in the same household or grown up together, you can (and likely will) have vastly different perspectives of the exact same situation. My mom has often struggled with this concept when she thinks about the differences between her and her brothers, frequently wondering how they could have shared so many similar experiences yet think so differently. I find her shock hysterical, not only because of their dynamics but also because no matter how I phrase these factors to her, she is still in disbelief. One is not better than the other, nor is any one approach good or bad; they're just different. My family is not the exception here. Narratives, beliefs, traditions, behaviors, and culture are all passed down and filtered through the eyes of the individual. How you integrate them into your sense of self and life are what differs.

All the factors of your family are then additionally influenced by societal and external messages. They combine to impact not only how you use your money but whether you feel you are able to handle and manage your money. If those messages (verbal, observed, or nonverbal) were positive, it can cultivate internal money confidence, but if those messages left you in the dark or did not provide a positive example, self-doubt is bound to creep in and thrive at some point. This is why representation is so important. It provides an example of possibility, even if you don't feel like you have all the tools yet. You know there is a path, a beacon, if you will, that says you can, too.

Seeing few images of people who look like you handling and managing money in a healthy way prevents children, and later adults, from feeling confident with money. While you learn about how to manage money well and work to meet your financial priorities, underlying feelings can be left unaddressed, and there is one system in particular that props up these thoughts and limiting beliefs far too often: patriarchy.

Many women and young girls have internalized the common tropes that money is solely about math and that girls in general are inherently bad at it. This false self-belief in conjunction with a lack of access to adequate, gender-neutral financial education leads so many people, specifically women, to give up managing their finances and leave it in the hands of those deemed most capable in their lives—often men. Literally no one is served by this narrative. Internalizing the belief that you are not good with money and doing nothing to remedy it can set you up for that very fate, resulting in a self-fulfilling financial prophecy.

This is a perfect example of how the narratives we are taught become our beliefs. "I am not good with math" is born from the same narrative as "If I don't look at it, it will go away." They are siblings cut from the same toxic, constricting cloth. It is a sad manifestation of the varying messages you received. They seep into your thoughts, becoming fact in your mind and sneakily integrating into the fabric of who you think you are. Throughout this book, we are going to interrupt this belief by exploring your past, identifying where you first heard and committed to false narratives, and shifting this old way of thinking into a more empowered thought and feeling. Being told or feeling like you are not good with math or numbers is less about what you are capable of and more about what you have been *taught* you aren't capable of.

More Money, More Problems?

Although most of my clients are navigating what it means to move up the economic ladder, this does not mean that people who start higher up get away without money wounds. Money is coveted as a universal problem solver in our country, but having money or growing up having it does not make you immune to problems. Toxic family dynamics and manipulation don't care how much money is in the bank. Money, in the form of inheritance or allowance, is often wielded to keep people in line or ensure they meet the family's expectations of what is acceptable. This can result in adult children having low self-esteem, being codependent, engaging in sibling rivalries, experiencing a loss of self, or realizing that they lived their life for someone other than themselves. This is a slow cooker recipe toward misery and depression. Now this is not to say that we need to shed tears for the wealthy instead of "eating them"—I'm just saying that wealthy people have problems because *people* have problems. No one can escape feeling pain or trauma in this life, no one. Fortunately for this group, they may have the resources to get the support they need or more time to deal with their issues fully, but their relationship with money is just as influenced by those around them and the unspoken rules of their family as it is for someone who doesn't have as much money.

To maintain their internal comfort, many people have become extremely accustomed to pushing past their traumatic experiences without allowing space for them to fully emotionally process it. Within my practice, I've noticed that feelings spurred by family dynamics are even further protected and unexplored. A major shift often occurs in sessions when my client is able to put aside how much they respect and love their family in order to admit that their childhood was hard. Knowing their family "did the best they could" or "didn't know any better" frequently gets in the way of being able to admit that although it was no one's fault, growing up felt hard and had a lasting impact. Helping my clients check their respect at the door is complex. The adult version of you may have the insight and maturity to recognize the effort of those who raised you, but the wounded child within you deserves space to feel validated in whatever feelings they had at the time.

To be clear, I am not giving my clients unfettered permission to be disrespectful, but I want to create a place where individuals can be truly honest. Respect and reverence can overshadow their ability to be honest about their feelings, and there is no room for that in my office. The space we create, physical or virtual, frequently serves as one of the only places my clients can learn and get comfortable expressing their most authentic self. It is difficult to admit your feelings, especially if there was never room, time, or encouragement to be vulnerable while growing up. Supporting my clients through this is a major part of my work, as I teach them it is okay to feel, to be, and to express themselves authentically. That is an act of vulnerability and rebellion in and of itself. Being hurt in the past seems to fuel people to retreat deeper into themselves, forcing their feelings down to a place they either do not know how to visit or stay as far away from as humanly possible. Then, without knowing it, those feelings rear their ugly heads when they are triggered by outside circumstances, manifesting in a myriad of ways, like spending money to cope with feelings.

For someone attempting to figure out their relationship with money, the popular belief that money will buy happiness can feel like a solution. I have a complicated relationship with this notion. On one hand, I know money can dramatically change lives for the better, providing stability, time, and access to care, treatment, and many other necessities, but there are limits. Up to a certain point money can buy happiness, but after that threshold is met, money may not be what's needed to bring the joy or happiness you crave. A recent study done by Killingsworth, Kahneman, and Meller updated the past research of Kahneman, which originally found that people reach the threshold of money happiness at $75,000. In other words, people would be no more or less happy after making $75,000. Their current research now suggests that income exceeding $500,000 shows no shift in overall happiness. They did state in their survey of over 33,000 people that they did not have as many people participating who were making over half a million dollars, which could very well skew these results, but the sentiment remains.[10]

While money can buy a ton of things that make life easier, more stable, comfortable, and safer, I know there are a lot of people with a ton of money who are absolutely miserable. Depression, anxiety, and trauma could not give two shits how much money you have. Of course, making more money can significantly change your life, but addressing the root of who you are, where you come from, and how all that impacts your mental health will always be necessary. This is why the core of this book is focused less on money-making strategies and more on understanding ourselves better. Simply filling your bank accounts will not heal you. You can't spend your way into true wellness. While adding a zero may feel nice for a moment, it won't matter if you haven't done the work to understand yourself and feel good about your relationship with money. If you are mismanaging $50,000, you will most certainly mismanage $150,000.

So far, we have walked through how the history of our families, collective trauma, upbringing, and lived experiences combine to form our money story, which then forms our mindset. This may or may not shift as you grow older, but it will always be a part of your story. Still, there are plenty of instances where we may not realize how our life experience impacts how we behave with money. I was a prime example of this.

My Money Story

I am from Albany, New York, but both of my parents were born and raised in New York City—my dad in Brownsville, Brooklyn, and my mom in Harlem then Jamaica, Queens. They made the move north after getting married and landing government jobs, and now they are both reaping the benefits of having what is now the rare diamond of retirement: a pension. What a life!

I grew up in what felt like a normal household, financially speaking. "Normal" being middle class for upstate New York. We lived in a house in downtown Albany, which had yet to be rebranded by gentrification into the Warehouse District and was less affectionately called Arbor Hill. It was a little hood but provided a great childhood for me. We had a brownstone that my parents loved because it reminded them of living in the city. However, despite their commitment to live in the city, the questionable happenings at the local elementary school led my parents to send both my brother and me to private Catholic schools about ten minutes across the Hudson River in the suburbs. Going to school there meant I was an out-of-district student. While us Albany kids got our books from school, the other kids who lived more locally got their books distributed at some pick-up site within the area. It didn't take me long to realize that in the suburbs, Albany was nearly synonymous with Black.

I did not always feel the impact of my racial identity at school, but I do remember in second grade that the kid I had a crush on said he couldn't like me because I was Black. He was immediately schooled by the other kids in our friend group about how that was biased and racist (we had just learned about the topic in class), but that didn't stop me from feeling bad. Ultimately, I let it slide. I was in second grade . . . I let everything slide then.

At school, living in Albany was considered "scary" compared to the quieter suburban life of so many of my counterparts. As a result, my white friends rarely came to my house; I always went to theirs. However, it didn't take long for the kids at my school to realize what our wealth looked like. We had three cars (two for everyday living and one for my dad's side business), and my parents always came to pick my brother and me up dressed in suits for their fancy government jobs, always smelling delightful. I remember being so upset that I had to stay for aftercare; what felt shitty to me as a little kid was simply being a product of two working parents. I didn't know it put me on the more financially privileged end of the spectrum. Looking back, the assumption about who we were as a Black family impacted my own understanding of my financial standing.

The kids at school assumed all the Black kids were either related or had crushes on each other, but this didn't feel like a big deal to me because my experiences outside of school were unequivocally Black. We went to a Black church, lived in a Black neighborhood, my parents had Black friends, and we vacationed in North Carolina to visit family or in Florida to be on the beach. A couple of times we even went to the coveted Martha's Vineyard (the Black part), and at least one to two weekends per month were spent in New York City visiting family. My brother and I seamlessly transitioned to being "real" city kids on the weekends. We would take the three-hour trip south and run around like Bebe's Kids with all my cousins, buying chips and bags of candy with the money our aunts and uncles would slip us. It was amazing.

My upbringing was exactly what it sounds like: privileged with a healthy mix of the realities of being Black in America. I still dealt with subtle acts of racism, like being followed in stores, the occasional neighborhood fight, and being consistently underestimated academically. My parents had a messy divorce when I was ten, but honestly, even that didn't really interrupt my sense of stability, financial or otherwise. This, I know, is a privilege.

Like many middle schoolers, it did not take me long to realize that buying and having the latest brands was a way for me to stamp my coolness. This was prime Limited Too, Adidas, Deb, and Abercrombie & Fitch era for all my geriatric millennials out there. Unsurprisingly, my mom was not interested in spending $40 for a fifth grader's jeans, but I was, and that was only the beginning. Despite one of my friends at school calling me a "ditz with a credit card" (Cher Horowitz would be proud), I felt like my family inherently had less, especially compared to the kids at the public school.

White Hot: The Rise & Fall of Abercrombie & Fitch, the 2022 Netflix documentary about the famed retailer, highlighted how the company marketed the store to feel exclusive not only in price but appearance.[11] Some of us may remember the intimidating, loud music and ever-present stench of cologne. I admit I fell victim to the marketing ploy, except there was a problem. My mom was not spending that kind of money on any one item of clothing for me, and I wasn't exactly their target audience. Every fiber in my youthful being told me that Abercrombie & Fitch was exactly what I needed to be cool and hot because when you are going through puberty in middle school, being pretty is social currency.

In hindsight, I recognize that I was trying to brand myself as "sought after," fresh, different, and yet the same all at once, when what I really felt was impossibly uncool. Like many teenagers then and now, I wanted to buy myself cool, to feel wanted, pretty, desired—all the things I thought I could find on the rack at Abercrombie & Fitch, Delia's, or Wet Seal. Poor baby Aja. I didn't feel like I met the standards of beauty, and to be honest, at that time I didn't. The standards of beauty I was comparing myself to and being compared to were white. Whether I had braids, cornrows, or moisture-fearing, chemically relaxed, pin-straight hair, I didn't feel like I was nailing it, but I naively thought it was just about the clothes.

I knew these feelings of inadequacy and low self-esteem were there, but like many teenagers, a part of me just thought it was about my hair and makeup, being too tall, or not having boobs or a butt. You know, teenage stuff. Don't get it twisted—on some level it *was* about a lot of that stuff. It's a hard age navigating who you are and how you feel about yourself, but another complicating factor was tokenism, which Danielle Prescod extensively defines in her debut memoir *Token Black Girl*. I had always given high school mixed reviews and recalled being called "token" for a week, but it wasn't until I read Prescod's definition that it really hit me.

Prescod wrote:

The Token Black Girl is characterized mostly by her proximity to her white peers and her nonthreatening and friendly nature. She is nonthreatening because she is almost never the romantic interest, and her primary function is to provide "attitude" and "sass," either as humor or as an attempt to elevate the sex appeal of the otherwise all-white-entity. She is a good student because she has to be. She actually feels like she has to be good at everything. She's almost always a good dancer, and even if she's not, it doesn't matter because everyone will still think she's a good dancer. She either has or can get the requisite social signifiers of acceptance—everything except white skin, of course. She will be well spoken, well dressed, and well groomed. She likes all the things her friends like, including boys, but they will not like her. She almost never acknowledges her position as the sole Black member of a group because talking about race makes white people uncomfortable. She can never make white people uncomfortable. Her most critical responsibility is providing protection against the "racist" label that might otherwise be hurled at a gaggle of white women devoid of ethnic variety.[12]

While I didn't fit every part of Prescod's description, a lot applied. That was me, the token Black girl, not in all aspects of my life but in enough spaces, usually academic, to have an impact. While I had had a financial awakening in my late twenties, reading her description nearly a decade later helped me further connect the dots of why I was spending the way I was in my early twenties. As a full-blown adult with children, I realized that throughout my life I was trying to buy myself cool. Baby Aja was trying to measure up to white standards of beauty by wearing Abercrombie jeans, and similarly, freshly minted, twenty-something New York City Aja was trying to keep up with brunches and happy hours. It wasn't just for everyone else; it was for me, too. That small burning feeling of potentially being inadequate was a soft spot of insecurity that triggered me. It was a financial trigger that hit my self-esteem like a wrecking ball, except now I had much more confidence and self-esteem. I was cool; I had fun; I went to amazing events, countless brunches, and traveled often—you name it. I had an amazing life. However, I did exactly what I had done since I started working at fifteen: I spent money trying to keep up. What I wish I could have told myself then is that there will always be more; what's most important is how you see yourself.

My spending highlighted the way I felt about myself in relation to those around me: "Please think I am cool, please include me, please know that I am valuable." I realized that whenever I felt insecure, I thought money would solve it; I wanted to cope by spending. In moments of distress, I would be immediately transported to that young girl who felt inadequate, who could justify swiping my card because if I just had, wore, spent, ate, or was at—fill in the endless blank—I would be awesome, and I would never be snubbed.

My interest in personal finance, born out of necessity to get my financial life together, fueled my passion to work toward bridging the gap between mental health and finances with financial therapy. My quest to better understand financial therapy principles allowed me to string together my own money story and money narratives. Don't get me wrong—sometimes I still catch myself wanting to spend my way out of a bad feeling—but I've learned some tools to help me navigate those emotions better (more on this later).

The point is, in my self-exploration, I realized I was doing the same thing to compensate for how I felt when I was younger. Talk about a mind fuck. I literally do this for a living and that connection escaped me until it came down on me like my declining credit score. I am happy to say that things are much better for me financially now, but that success did not come until I started looking at what and how I was spending. For me, first came financial education and then came connecting my history, life, and feelings to my spending. It is still hard to say no to the things I want—I know I am not alone in that—but at least now I can pinpoint why I am doing it.

I am aware of how my main financial triggers show up in how I make purchases, not just for me but for my children. They are young, so I am not in the thick of it yet, but I know how hard puberty and teenage years can be on all parties involved. I would be lying if I didn't say there are times when I want to make sure my kids have "cool" things because of how I felt in the past. There is a part of me that wants to protect them from, well, everything, even though I know that is not possible. In an effort to shield them from one less bruised feeling, worry, teasing session, or bully, I would happily buy the goods. But I also know I want to raise children who aren't defined by what they are wearing, what they have or don't, or how other people rate them based on materialism. However, because it is still a struggle for me not to want to keep up with the Joneses, I know this is going to be a place of growth for me as a parent. My baggage will be triggered in their life experiences. Woof! It is my job to contain my emotional baggage as much as possible to nurture and care for them, all while nourishing who they will become, giving them space to be themselves, and continuing to learn about myself and heal my own wounds. Parenting ain't easy.

The stories you hear and absorb can so quickly become the stories you believe. Those narratives have roots, and your emotions can be completely intertwined in them. The strategies and skills you needed to survive when you were young may no longer be needed as an adult. You may not see how those beliefs are tangled in your financial behaviors and habits right now, but that is what this book is for: to help you recognize, explore, feel, and understand yourself, your money narrative, and your money beliefs so you can create change and move toward your financial goals in a healthier way. The tools in this book will teach you to honor your past as you replace old skills with those better suited for where you currently are in your life and free you from your past money mistakes with a new commitment to move forward with grace and understanding. As you read, I encourage you to think deeply, take notes, and let the emotions come. It's okay if you shed some tears; it is all a part of your growth.

Reflection Questions

Reflect on how money was used by the adults around you in childhood. These experiences shape how you see money used to fix, hide, shift, or cope with hardships.

- How did your family cope with hard situations?
- What coping skills do you think you adopted from how you were raised?
- Was spending money used as a way to shift the mood? If so, how?
- Did you witness the yo-yoing of having money, spending it on whatever, and then swinging back to a place of lack?

Chapter 3

Your Psychological Context

Incredible women are everywhere. She's listening to a romance novel on the train, dropping her baby off at daycare before heading to the office, excelling as the exec on the stage, and even fulfilling her dreams of traveling as the rich (monetarily or otherwise) auntie. Women are constantly setting examples for people in and around their orbit of what it means to show up and be bold. Sadly, this beacon of strength isn't always celebrated in the way we deserve. While powerhouses like Viola Davis, Shonda Rhimes, and Issa Rae provide beautiful examples of what it means to be strong, successful, and brave enough to stand in your power, the relatability of these women owning their respective industries can be lost in what feels like an unobtainable fantasy of celebrity. Don't get me wrong—we know they had to bust their asses to get where they are, and that did not happen overnight. We also know these women are extremely important to the cause of lifting up and supporting other Black women; however, having a tangible, realistic path to follow is also important. The representation and modeling of a "normal" person (rather than a celebrity) becoming wealthy and reaching new heights helps provide an inner sense of possibility for those of us with less-than-glamorous lives.

I am privileged enough to have had examples in family members, especially my mom, and friends who provided me with Black representations of financial stability. Outside of those relatable middle-class models, though, images of Black success and, more specifically, Black wealth were lacking. This is most likely what provided me with the beginnings of my motivation to grind to *be* that representation. The lowered expectations of what I was capable of or who I would be simply because I was Black implanted a will inside of me that, at this point, can be bruised, but is virtually indestructible. I know this is true for many people who look like me; we work hard despite those lowered expectations, which can certainly impact how we see ourselves and our capabilities.

When I talk with my friends and clients, many of them cite their mom as a model for their foundational values. I am no different. My mom served as an example of what was achievable and laid the foundation for who I am. Her dreamer nature instilled a level of belief, some might say delusional levels, that I truly could achieve anything I put my mind to. Because of her, I was manifesting before I knew the meaning of the word, dreaming up my ideal scenarios, cultivating them, and doing my best to execute them whenever possible. It took me a while to buy in to her faith in my ability to shift what seemed impossible to possible, but I believe her now. It was difficult to hone, but this faith in my abilities comes from my unwavering dedication to do literally anything in my power to make shit happen! That is how we got here, with this book in your hands.

Unwavering faith and ambition do have a cost, though. It can affect your relationships with those around you and impact your own sense of self. Shifts in economic status (in either direction) can trigger a multitude of emotional reactions, including guilt and shame. And, in addition to the historical and personal contexts we discussed in chapter 2, there's a psychological context we also need to contend with, and that's what we'll explore here.

In this chapter, we'll examine some common reactions and responses to money and wealth within the community context. We'll talk about shame and guilt in your money stories and cover the four types of money scripts. We'll close by exploring the role of social media and finding the balance between comparison and representative visibility. Interestingly, all these social and interpersonal reactions aren't a matter of environmental or sociocultural factors. In fact, they are rooted in neuroscience and psychology. Let's begin by exploring the place where this all begins, a little closer to home than we may have realized: our own brains.

We're Hardwired for This

Even when we understand the brain's complexities, unknowns, and vastness, we still struggle with the fact that each of us is so greatly impacted by our experiences. Regardless of whether you've gone through the same thing as someone else, no two people will have the exact same perspective. How you perceive, internalize, and process your experiences will always be different. Even when we look at twins, we find that although they have identical DNA, life experience and perception always create nuance for each individual.

During the times of hunting and gathering, we needed to rely on one another as a matter of survival—safety in numbers. Community meant home and that your needs would be met, while being ostracized from the group was not only tortuous but also a matter of life and death. The chances of survival were much lower when you were alone. Those instincts are still within us; they just manifest in different ways now. But I've found that in our modern, individualistic society, we have forgotten how important being in community is to our survival. Swinging the pendulum too far away from relying on one another has left many people feeling isolated and lonely. The decline in US multigenerational living started in the 1950s and bottomed out around 1960.[13] In episode seventy-six of *The Money with Katie Show*, host Katie Gatti Tassin highlights the reality that although moving out at a young age (eighteen to twenty-two) feels like the norm in the United States, it very much isn't in other parts of the world. Cohabitating for longer periods of time with multiple generations is common for many cultures. (I am looking at you, my glorious people of color.) Additionally, since the Great Recession in 2008 we've seen the previous decrease in multigenerational living boomerang back toward increasing numbers. Unfortunately, spending time in one another's company has too frequently been reduced to sitting next to each other while silently scrolling on the phone. It's giving *WALL-E*. Humans are shockingly inherently community based, but we have continued to push ourselves into believing that, as individuals, being vulnerable or needing help is in some way harmful or a weakness.

Let's pause here for a brief neuroscience lesson. Trauma of Money (TOM) is a sixteen-week online program focused on understanding financial education through the lens of bringing together the psychology of trauma, scarcity, and our relationship with money. The program takes participants on an experiential journey of understanding how lived experiences, whether involving money or not, have potentially impacted our relationship with money. TOM describes what happens in our brain when we react to a threat: (1) the basal ganglia, which are where our bodily reactions, instincts, and impulses live; (2) the limbic system, where our emotional understanding, responses, and implicit memory originate from; and (3) the frontal cortex, where intellect, executive functioning, reasoning, language, conscious thought, and self-awareness are housed.[14] It is important to understand that the same process takes place in our brain when we perceive any kind of threat, whether it's a tornado heading toward our home or a financial threat like a looming recession. Our perception of these threats ultimately impacts what we choose to do to respond to the threat appropriately. Fortunately, our instincts are designed to keep us alive with the fight-or-flight response. To keep it simple, when our brains become aware of a threat, our frontal cortex quiets, our filters of reasoning, conscious thought, and self-awareness are removed, and our basal ganglia prepare for action. This process gets particularly complicated when we add the complexities of trauma, but we will discuss that later.

Money and Community

So, what does this all have to do with our money? Now that we understand the dire importance of community and what happens to our brain when we are threatened, let's walk through how these components show up in everyday life.

Take a moment to think about all the communities you have belonged to in your lifetime: at home, in school, on teams, in the neighborhood, at work, in your social life, and so on. Money, among other things, is one way people can be seen as different within these communities. Drs. Brad and Ted Klontz are pioneers in the financial psychology space and have written multiple foundational books on the subject. In their book *Mind Over Money*, they discussed the "crab-barrel effect" as a means of demonstrating that people want to stay within their communities of origin and that the communities of origin want people to stay within the confines of what they consider the norm. The Klontzes describe how, when crabs are caught and placed in a barrel, there always seems to be a few crabs who are hell-bent on escaping, clawing their way to the top in an effort to get out, but inevitably they are pulled back down by others. This is no different than how humans interact with one another, especially when finances are concerned.[15]

A few years ago, I was listening to HOT 97's morning show when the hosts were discussing the untimely death of rapper Young Dolph and the frequency with which things like this happen to so many young artists, athletes, and first-generation wealth builders as they come up from their modest upbringings. These artists typically come from tough, traumatic lives and are simultaneously shifting away from that lifestyle and gaining fame for sharing what they lived through. But what happens to their roots, the ties of a life they lived so vividly? Often, these ties become rotted with jealousy of perceived wealth, whether that person is truly doing better or not. It can be hard for community members to accept someone else's success when their own life feels so fucking far from that. This is the human form of the crab in the barrel.

Now, I am not sitting too far away in a palace of privilege to understand how awful it is to feel like positive things only happen to other people and never you. This is a shitty way to feel. It crushes self-esteem and motivation and frequently pisses people off. I know I have felt that way. It is hard to watch others succeed when you feel like there is absolutely no way you will get to that point. These feelings can often lead people to pull others down, whether that person was trying to bring others up with them or invest in the community.

People do not want to be iced out of their communities, regardless of their financial position, and those feelings of perceived loneliness not only impact us psychologically, increasing anxiety, depression, and suicidal ideation, but also physically. As we know, humans are not meant to live in prolonged states of stress.[16] It is just not good for our overall well-being. Remaining positively connected to one's roots and community serves the person who has shifted just as much as those within the community; it's mutually beneficial. That said, the fear of social isolation can often govern financial behaviors.

In addition to artists, successful athletes and first-generation wealth builders are often forced to navigate wealth in a manner that requires examining who they are and who they want to be, a sort of identity shift. This calls for them to learn how to make room for their new life and experiences with more money while holding on to the roots of their foundation.

To avoid this crab-in-a-barrel mentality, we must shift the way we think about individual success and failure in this modern society, and language is an important part of reclaiming this new narrative. Many of us may often use terms like *broke* and *poor* to describe their financial situation, but I think the way we use them can have a strong impact on us psychologically, even if we don't realize it. To me, being broke is having enough to take care of your basic needs, and perhaps a few small wants here and there, but also having times when you struggle to make ends meet. On the other hand, being poor implies there is a constant struggle to get all your needs met. There is no room for extra. I know people generally don't like to claim these words, but they are, in fact, the reality of too many of us. *Broke* is not a dirty word; it is simply the hard truth.

James Grubman, author of *Strangers in Paradise*, uses the analogy of immigrating to a new place as a way to understand people who have shifted economic status and adapted to a new way of life. He specifically discusses three ways in which people respond to acquired personal wealth. The first is avoidance or separation, clinging tightly to the culture of their roots with an "emphasis on retaining middle- or working-class attitudes, beliefs, behaviors, adopting little of the alien and/or presumably toxic culture of affluence."[17] An example of this might look like someone who purposefully never changes their life after they receive money. They might buy the same reasonably priced cars, shop at the same budget stores, or even purchase a modest home in an average neighborhood. This can be really good for living below your means or building your own wealth, but there is a difference between healthy money moves and detrimental ones. The desire to reject the money can lead to feelings of guilt and shame for having resources that others in the community may not, and it can cause a scarcity mindset, where people hoard their money in checking accounts without trying to grow it. It may seem like frivolously giving money away or refraining from utilizing it at all would be helpful, but the problem with these extreme approaches is that the person may not allow themselves to freely use their money in a way that makes their life easier and benefits their community.

The second is assimilation—completely abandoning the values and behaviors they once lived and diving headfirst into living and acting the part. This one in particular is a surefire way to blow your money quickly, if you ask me. This may look like someone completely disregarding the values and principles of their past lifestyle and acting like those things are now beneath them and not worth their time, energy, or attention. You know, acting brand new.

And last, integration intertwines the foundation of your past values and beliefs with the practicality of the benefits and comfort you are now able to afford.[18] An example of this can be seen in Will Smith's character on *The Fresh Prince of Bel-Air*. While Will had his struggles living in Bel-Air, by the end of the show, he grew to understand that he was capable of more than he had given himself credit for. He decided to stay in

California and finish his schooling, all while understanding that he may not have even made a choice to go to college in the first place if he hadn't moved. He remained true to himself and the values his mom, Vy, and West Philadelphia instilled in him while integrating the privileges afforded to him by his aunt and uncle. This kind of inner work isn't easy, but it's possible.

This acclimation to a new way of living and being is directly connected to our instinct of belonging. What once served as a means of survival is turned on its head when you are now in a place to decide which tribe you belong to. It can be heart-breaking to shift away from people, places, and attitudes you've known all your life, even when your intention is to include them in the new things in your life, but sadly, people aren't always willing to accept the new changes in your life, even if they were supporting and pushing you to get there all along. People love an underdog story, especially when it comes to overcoming harsh circumstances, but those same fans can very quickly turn on underdogs when the original story shifts from one that looked similar to theirs to one of abundance and wealth. People love to watch others rise and win, but if their winnings are too big, people will try to bring them back down. It's toxic.

Money, Shame, and Guilt, Oh My!

Change takes time and is often fraught with emotional tur-moil, which is probably why so many people dread shifting their life, even if it is for the better. I used to use the analogy of cleaning out your closet to demonstrate the process of change: Sometimes things have to get messy before you are able to put everything back in a more organized way. Even when you feel like your life is messy, the messy you know is often more comfortable than the messy you don't know. When there is a significant change in economic status, feelings of guilt and shame can be quick to appear.

Guilt and shame are two emotions that frequently get confused. The way I describe it to clients is that guilt is feeling like you did something bad, like accidentally bumping into someone on your way out the door, while shame is feeling like you are a bad person because of your actions. Using the same example, feeling shame for bumping into someone means you feel like that bump makes you a bad person. As you can imagine, this mindset is often accompanied by harsh self-talk. While chatting with Stefanie O'Connell Rodriguez on *Real Simple*'s *Money Confidential* podcast, Tiffany "the Budgetnista" Aliche said, "Shame is a liar; shame doesn't say there was a mistake that was made, shame says you are a mistake. You feel bad about yourself versus focusing on an action you have control over."[19]

Like any other kind of shame, financial shame—feeling like you are a bad person because of your money moves, mistakes, or regrets—can impact how you engage with the rest of the world. Feeling bad about not sticking to your budget, being in debt, not knowing how to shift your financial circumstances, or not being in a position to go on vacation with your girls are all examples of how financial shame can manifest. It breeds isolation and can, subsequently, eat away at your self-esteem. I have been there, as I mentioned in chapter 1, trying to hide my concerns over my finances by spending even more when I had no business doing so. I felt a lot of financial shame for not being able to pay for things with the seeming ease of some of my peers. It's a tough feeling to deal with, and our tendency is to stay quiet about it when we feel it, but to shake shame, you have to share it. Give voice to the things you are ashamed about because it often thrives in your isolation and negative self-talk.

On the podcast *So Money with Farnoosh Tarobi*, Tarobi coined her own negative inner voice the "shitty committee." What we need to do is fire our shitty committees. We keep them employed simply because we are used to them. Negative self-talk quickly becomes a habit in how we react to being stressed, essentially shaming ourselves as if it is going to motivate us to do better, but I am going to give it to you straight: This doesn't work! It is a recipe for feeling bad about yourself, and despite what you may think, it doesn't make you feel better or promote change. You know what *does* help? Talking to someone you feel safe around. This starts the process of breaking down shame and feelings of isolation. Finding out that you are, in fact, not the only person having these feelings can help shift your perspective past your being a bad person. In fact, you may be surprised at how validated and relieved you feel by getting those negative feelings off your chest, whether it's with a family member, friend, financial advisor, or therapist.

If you take away anything from this chapter, let it be this: When we feel like we are truly seen by others, understood, and accepted, we thrive. Humans want to be intimate and in community with one another, and communicating our deepest shameful secrets in supportive spaces is a great way to reinforce these ties. It reminds us that we are not alone, that we are worthy, deserving, and enough despite the mistakes we may have made in the past.

Reflection Questions

- When was the first time you felt shame about your financial situation?
- Did this shame shift the way you interacted with others?
- In what ways has financial shame hindered the way you show up socially?

Now, when it comes to money, shame and guilt are the emotional royalty in the land of negativity, most likely because taboo shit makes us feel bad when we don't talk about it, and money is just one of those things people tend to keep private. While that is usually okay to do, that does not mean it needs to be a secret. We all have to navigate money, whether you are spending, saving, or giving it, but the way we skirt around the topic makes it seem as if it doesn't have a ubiquitous position in our society. I like to believe people avoid money conversations in an effort to be respectful or polite, not wanting to cause harm to others who may not be in the same financial situation as them, but this secrecy has driven a massive stake into our comfort and trust in one another, pushing us away from being open about money and further driving isolation and shame. This is demonstrated very well in the way employees are discouraged from speaking openly about their salaries. Keeping these kinds of conversations secret benefits no one but the company because when employees aren't up front with each other about what they make, companies never have to worry about pay equity, thus keeping many people potentially making less than they should.

The interesting part about all of this is that people often feel financial guilt and shame regardless of whether they have a ton of money or not, whether they've worked incredibly hard to earn it or not. Money does not care who you are or what you do to obtain it, but people certainly do. We assign value to ourselves and others too frequently based upon what is in someone's bank account and how it got there, judging them based on their net worth and career instead of their self-worth. It is part of the human condition to care about what people think of you. Remember, we all want to be seen, accepted, and welcomed into the community. But there is a difference between accepting that others may judge you, which is laced with the context of their life's experience, and shifting how you live your life based on said judgment.

Often, those complex desires for belonging can be financially problematic if you are not in a financial position to provide a certain lifestyle for yourself, your family, and potentially the community. I tell the story often about when I started making a certain amount of money and my mom told me she would be handing her phone bill over to me. It wasn't a big deal, and I could afford it, but it was most definitely her expectation. I was raised on it, I knew what it was, and if I were ever in a similar position, I would be provided some support as well. To be clear, my mom is in a very financially stable place. She is doing just fine with her retirement earnings and savings and lives a comfortable life. It was more about the expectation that so many of us in communities of color are raised with. I have no qualms about it, and I know a lot of us are more than happy to financially provide for those who raised us, but this can be hard to manage. Do you really have the money to share? Are you taking away from your household or goals to meet your obligations of respect? Do you even want to give? Family dynamics have a way of bringing up a ton of emotions—pride, anger, sadness, anxiety, shame, and guilt.

This is only further complicated when your goals and your family's desires for support are not aligned.

The expectation to help the family is not as detrimental when you can afford it, and I want to make it clear that no one should be hurting themselves financially in order to create generational wealth. I know this may be controversial, and I am certainly not telling you to avoid helping out Grandma if she is struggling. Please do that if that makes you happy; however, it is important to set healthy boundaries around what you can and can't do in order to be able to handle your responsibilities for your future self and family. You could set a certain amount of money aside in a separate account or within your account and give from there until that is exhausted. Then it's up to you to start saying no. You could also offer to pay for whatever your family member needs directly versus sending or handing over cash. Or you can start off giving a low amount, then slowly increase it over time as you become comfortable and stable with your finances. Take the time to devise a plan that works to provide for those you love while keeping your financial goals in mind. Admittedly, setting boundaries around money is extremely difficult, and knowing that others may not respect them makes it even harder. So, for some, it could feel more comfortable to quickly spend their money so they don't have enough to give to family instead of saying no, which can further perpetuate unhealthy relationships with money.

The Money Scripts Theory

While we're here, I have a quick note for my intellectual girlies who like to get into the nitty-gritty of it all. If you want to get a bit more theoretical with this work, Drs. Ted and Brad Klontz developed four money scripts that have served as the theoretical foundation in our understanding of finances and psychology. Money scripts, as the Klontzes define them, are unconscious core beliefs we have about money that govern how we think, feel, and behave with it. They include money avoidant, money status, money vigilance, and money worship.

Money avoidance: This is when you knowingly or unknowingly avoid dealing with money, rejecting any responsibility for finances (think ignoring your statements or rarely checking your credit card balance). There is often extreme anxiety when it comes to financial tasks.

Money status: This is the notion that your self-worth is equal to your net worth. These people believe they are only as successful as the amount of money they have, thus money gives them status. People who hold this script are more concerned with the outward displays of wealth than they are with the actual accumulation of money (see money worship). A more extreme person with this money script may say, "If you don't have the latest and greatest, then you must not have any money." This may also manifest in them buying things to show, signify, or appear like they are in a better financial position than they actually are.

Money vigilance: This script is representative of people who are extremely concerned about what is happening with their money. They may be discreet about it or wary of others when it comes to money. Excessive worry may keep them from enjoying their money or spending it on things that bring them joy.

Money worship: This person believes that happiness is found in the next raise, salary bump, or material item. This is the rat race personified and celebrated. The more money this person has, the more powerful they feel, which they believe will lead them to happiness. This can lead to excessive belief in hustle culture, chronic spending, compulsive buying, materialism, and an obsession with their financial success.[20]

Even though I know you are now sitting there analyzing which script sounds like you, I want to be clear that there is no right or wrong way to be. I begrudgingly find myself falling into the money status category. This information is less about judging yourself and more about identifying how your script shows up in your spending habits. The goal here is to find balance in your financial life.

Representation Matters

At the beginning of this chapter, we discussed what our communities likely looked like back in the hunter-gatherer days, and it comes as no surprise that, today, they look extremely different. Each day, we carry handheld computers that give us virtually limitless access to information and entertainment; you can get practically anything with a few clicks or swipes of the finger. No wonder we have issues with immediate gratification.

Social media started as a means to create connection and community with people around our age, but over the past couple of decades, it has ballooned into a way of life, completely shifting not only what we see but how and when we see it. Whole industries have been completely turned on their heads with apps and platforms that sell us the idea that, through their technology, we can connect with anyone. They were right, and the growth was exponential.

As technology and access shifted, so did, of course, the way we use them. Picture sharing on social media gave us a peek behind the curtain of how other people lived. Whether you were in a faraway country, right around the corner, or rich, poor, or somewhere in between, you were able to share your world with others. In social media's infancy, most of what you saw was raw and true to life, but as they say, the only constant is change, and when provided with tools we will use them. Nowadays, manipulating the appearance of your life has never been easier, and as a result, we are consuming more and more unrealistic content than ever before but comparing ourselves to it all the same.

This level of comparison can be a hot-button trigger that hits us where we feel most vulnerable. As that vulnerability bubbles up, we falsely believe that the quick fix of spending on material goods and attaining what we see on the screen will make us feel better. Often people think of their past when the topic of scarcity is brought up. They think about potentially having to go without as a child and the stressors and traumas that resulted because of it. You may not always remember every detail of the experience, but intense emotions are often attached to life-altering financial situations. It's almost like it sears itself into your memory bank, even if the moments leading up to it or directly after are fuzzy.

This is all valid, but that learned scarcity mindset can impact your present as well. When we feel as though other people are doing things we aren't, whether it be via comparison or just witnessing, we can quickly begin to wonder if we are "normal." Remember, one of our strongest human urges is to be in community with and accepted by others. Despite social media platforms being a virtual community of strangers, it is still a community, and one that serves a strong purpose. We celebrate society's outliers for daring to be different, but we don't necessarily want to be one. It can be incredibly lonely being different. This is why social media was so amazing in the first place. It provided a community for people with varied interests to come together and share them without being in physical proximity to one another. But humans are hardwired to compare ourselves to one another. Instead of solely connecting with each other based on our similarities, we very quickly start picking apart our differences, wondering why someone is "in such great shape," for example, while we are scrolling, asking ourselves how they can afford to have a better wardrobe, why their makeup looks cleaner, and what they're doing to have such an amazing life compared to ours. This kind of negative comparison, coupled with a scarcity mindset, has led people to feel bad about their reality when comparing it to the highlight reel of someone else. This mode of thinking has a sneaky way of hurting our self-esteem over time, and one way many people cope with this is by spending money on things that will ease the pain. Whether it's the dopamine rush of buying new clothes or yummy food, spending has become one of Americans' favorite ways to cope with how we feel. To be honest, this behavior is encouraged, but we will talk more about that later.

This is where the problem with technology lies. The peek behind the curtain gives us a view of what we can be, but it can be hard to differentiate between seeing what we *can be* and seeing what we (think we) *should have*. Although we can share our lives with others in positive, healthy ways, we have also collectively begun to curate what we want others to see and potentially think about us to gain more clicks and follows. We are "allowed" to see how others "live," even when their online life doesn't reflect what is truly going on. You see what someone chooses to show you, which is typically all the good stuff and none of the bad, hard, or ugly that it may have taken to get there. We see our favorite travel influencer's trip to Bali but not the credit card debt crushing them to make those trips look dreamy. We see the smiling couple on a date but not the arguments and frustrations at home. We all know this intellectually, but we fall victim to the trap of comparison frequently.

If comparison is the thief of joy, then social media is the getaway car. In the past, if you didn't have access to the details of someone else's life, it was pretty hard to compare yourself to them and impulse buy as a result. You could fantasize or imagine what they may be doing or purchasing, but you didn't know for sure unless they told you themselves. This is no longer the case. We now have a front-row seat to the lives of others and are a part of people's everyday lives in a way that didn't exist thirty years ago.

The need for community is written on the fabric of what it means to be human, and the narratives of your money beliefs are dependent on how you were taught and shown to handle it throughout your life. You may not be able to write your instincts, but you can rewrite and rewire the messaging you received around money. This is why representation and education are so important. Keep in mind, though, that there's a fine line between representation and comparison. There's a difference between saying, "I see myself in that person, so I know I can be that, too," and "I need what that person has in order to feel good about myself."

In that same episode of HOT 97's morning show I mentioned earlier, the hosts discussed Big Pun and Fat Joe going back to the projects they were from to talk to the kids. They said that Big Pun would roll up in his nice car to let the young kids know that they could get there, too. While I understand the reasoning behind that, I also wonder how different the kids' perception of him would be if he was driving a Toyota Corolla instead. Would they have the same respect? Regardless, representation matters, and modeling is how we learn. If you have never seen anyone who looks like you do something you want to do, it can be hard to envision yourself there. Not impossible, but definitely harder. This is why beauty standards should include different shades, hair textures, body types, and gender expressions. To collectively heal these divisive wounds we've inherited, we must begin to include as many people (shit, everyone!) as possible in the mainstream to foster innate confidence. You can write a book, you can be a professional athlete, you can be a lawyer, and you can have a healthy, productive, self-enhancing relationship with money. Representation matters.

Just ask Rihanna and Fenty Beauty, her billion-dollar company.

Reflection Questions

- During your childhood, how did you see the people around you interacting with money?
- How has the community (family, school, church, location, etc.) you were raised in impacted how you behave with your money?

Chapter 4

If I Don't Look at It, It Will Go Away

Now that we've established the importance of your per-sonal, historical, and psychological contexts and we have a better understanding of how our money narratives are created, the next step is exploring how these stories impact our money mindset and relationship with money over time. After all, we don't just wake up one day comparing ourselves to others, keeping our head in the sand, or hoarding our money. The understanding we have about money is completely rooted in our past experiences and the way we've been interacting with and hearing about it our entire lives.

Over the next few chapters, we're going to explore five common limiting beliefs around money and how these mindsets manifest themselves in our financial behavior. For each mindset, we'll explore some of the feelings that arise with it and the ways it shows up in our day-to-day lives. We'll also begin adding actionable tools into our financial wellness tool kit with each chapter. By the end of this exploration, you'll be equipped with a step-by-step guide to true financial wellness.

We'll start here with one of the most common money mindsets: If I don't look at it, it will go away. They say knowledge is power and knowing everything about your full financial picture is the first, albeit sometimes uncomfortable, step to great financial wellness.

Playing Ostrich

Are you attempting to go through life by ignoring one of the most important parts of it? Are you finding every excuse in the book not to open that bill? Are you watching your mail pile up for fear of what is inside one of those nondescript white envelopes? Are you avoiding looking at your bank account? Financial avoidance is an attempt to cope with the stress of money by pretending it isn't an issue, essentially hoping that if you don't look at it, it will just go away. Folks with this avoidant behavior often hope that somehow, magically, all their fears will fade away because things weren't addressed or they "didn't know." Sadly, this method frequently leaves people feeling even more stressed, as their sentiments of "I will get to it later" never actually come to fruition. Late fees, negative compounding interest, and collections, oh my! This is no way to cope, my friends. You and I both know it only makes things worse.

Avoidance in general is a coping mechanism used to escape, distract, or manage feelings of discomfort. The discomfort we are trying to manage can come from anything, including trauma, an unfavorable situation, negative feelings, judgment, or an uncomfortable environment. Similar to being triggered, avoidance can be your learned way of regulating your feelings or the potential for discomfort. As we discussed, family dynamics and modeling play a huge role in how we operate as adults, so if you identify with this behavior, it's very possible that this is a pattern you learned from watching the adults in your life navigate conflict in this way.

The thing about human behavior is that we use what we know. It doesn't matter what part of our life it applies to. When you've found a strategy that works and makes you feel better (however temporary), you will utilize that strategy over and over until you consciously replace it with another. The way you might avoid conflict with a person to save yourself from an uncomfortable conversation is the same way you may avoid dealing with money to avoid feelings of stress and anxiety. Money is simply another aspect of life you have to manage that may cause you stress, but burying your head in the sand (or desiring to) in hopes that your money problems will resolve themselves pretty much never works. What it does do is build even more shame, isolation, stress, and anxiety. Woof!

The stress and anxiety that comes from avoiding money can arise for a variety of reasons, but a few that apply far too frequently are lack of experience, opportunity, and information. Time for another history lesson. Before the year 1100 (yes, we are going that far back), women in western civilizations were "allowed" to own and inherit property. It wasn't until the 1100s that the financial rights of women began to be rolled back in favor of women being joined to men as one financial entity through marriage. That's right, ladies, the Powers That Were wanted both parties to operate as one (or really, women to be dependent on men), so our rights were taken away. Of course, the notion of joining as one financial entity through marriage was quickly corrupted further by patriarchy, leading to women themselves, as well as the finances, being looked at as the property of the husband.

This absurd way of thinking continued for a disgusting amount of time, and honestly, it still pervades today. While there have been small wins for women, such as the ability to own property through inheritance, list our names on a patent, and not be liable for the debts of a husband, modern-day financial necessities like the ability to open bank accounts (1960s), the right to "equal" pay (1963), and access to credit (1974) took a long time to come to fruition.[21] And the struggle is even more extensive for women of color. Even with more equitable policies in place, women's ability to independently navigate their finances was complicated by those who refused to honor the mandates. This was the foundation, among many other details, of what has gone into the gender wealth gap and the general lack of financial literacy many women find themselves living with.

Narratives like "Don't worry about it, honey, your husband will take care of it," "Go to college to meet an engineering student," or "Don't worry your little heart about it" were all commonplace refrains from our mothers, grandmothers, and most definitely our great-grandmothers. These beliefs and many others had an impact on both how women have been invited to the proverbial financial table and internalized misguided thoughts, such as that women aren't good at math or shouldn't worry about money. Generations of women were raised to believe they had to rely on a man for financial stability, and a lot of times they weren't "allowed" to do so for themselves. This has led many generations of women down the self-destructive path of financial avoidance.

A brief note: In this chapter, I'm focusing on those of us socialized as women because of the vast history of women being left out of the financial education game. While money avoidance can come into play in a variety of ways (we touch on entrepreneurship, as an example) for a variety of gender expressions, our focus here will be on money and traditional gender roles. However, money mindsets are universal, so please take what resonates with your lived experience and leave the rest on the shelf.

Picture This

You met him at a friend's graduation party your senior year. Although the intention wasn't to peruse your dating options, you were shocked to have spent four years at the same school without ever noticing him. He was right on time. After what felt like years of dating emotionally unavailable, noncommunicative men—being ghosted and wondering if he really liked you—you finally found someone you were truly excited about. You two got along great, and you felt like not only did you work well as a couple, but also you could work as life partners. You've always wanted children, so finding a mate wasn't only about your connection but also how you could operate together as parents.

You started dating, and two years later, he proposed. You were getting everything you thought you wanted. Things would be good now, easier. Going through life partnered was not only what the world told you to do but also what you felt like would continue to cement you in adulthood. It was all coming together.

Until it wasn't.

You were not 100 percent sure when or how things started to decline, but there was a stark difference in how you two treated each other after four children. He wasn't the partner in parenting you thought he would be. Instead, he was far more traditional and much more committed to gender roles than you. You went to work, took care of the kids, and managed the everyday household needs while he went to work and managed the finances and big decisions for the family. You weren't 100 percent comfortable with not being involved in the finances, but you couldn't pinpoint why, and you didn't feel like you understood enough about it to do what needed to be done with it. You were always taught to combine your money with your husband, so you did. The two of you slipped into your roles so easily, it didn't feel like a conscious decision. You showed up for your family but never managed to be there for one another. There was a chasm between you.

After years of trying to make it all work, you made the heartbreaking decision to separate and move toward a divorce. It was difficult but necessary. No one was happy. Things started out amicably, until you found out about the money or lack thereof. Of course, you two weren't rolling in the dough, but there was enough to keep the lights on and everyone fed. There had always been ups and downs, but he made it work. Little did you know that he had been completely mismanaging the finances. There was no savings account for the kids, barely any savings in general, and unbeknownst to you, your husband had made a series of bad investments with friends. What you didn't know, because you never asked or looked for yourself, was that he had no idea what he was doing, either.

You had been left in the dark and taken advantage of, and you felt awful. How could you have let it get so bad?

Thinking back on it, your husband had always acted like you were incapable of handling the money. You truly had no clue what to do, so he wasn't wrong. He had convinced you that he was taking care of everything. He said things were tight financially, but it always worked out. He had always said you didn't need to worry about it, so you didn't. It wasn't until the divorce when you realized just how important it was for you to know what was going on financially, and by then, it was too late. The damage had been done.

All the Feels: What We Don't Know

Unfortunately, this is a common experience. Those who blindly uphold the patriarchy (no, it is not only men) have either put themselves in or have benefited from being put in a position where they control or manage the money. There are times when this is intentional and times when a gender role may have been assigned without a thought of whether the person was equipped to handle the task. Outside of people who identify as women (more on the queer community soon) and how we are typically taught about money, men are often expected to know about personal finance with or without any structured education. The same way women have had to deal with money narratives being placed on them, so do men. Do not get me wrong, it is different. One way is far more damaging, but this isn't to say there aren't consequences from feeling that pressure. People are attempting to cope with the weight of responsibility, whether they have a deeper understanding of money and personal finance or not. We also know that society has often made it difficult for anyone to admit when they don't know something. This is further complicated when we layer in the impact of vulnerability. Because our society doesn't celebrate it, we tend to not make space for people to be honest when they need help. Toxic masculinity, the belief that manliness and masculinity are associated with certain attitudes or guidelines, and patriarchy serve no one. It is a lose-lose situation for all.

This is why I often urge my clients to discuss money with their partners as soon as possible so they can get vulnerable and openly talk about one of the most taboo, secretive topics of the modern human experience. Communication is at the foundation of any connection; communication provides an opportunity for you to get closer and a lack thereof drives a wedge that can feel like an abyss of emotion, silence, and misinterpreted glances. There is no need to do that to yourself or the other person when talking about it openly and honestly allows you to move forward and attune to the needs of each other, which will only make you stronger.

Queer Money

There are many identities people hold that have been used against them, too frequently impacting how they are able to move through the world. Queerness is one such identity. Pay discrepancies within the queer community are similar to race and gender wage gaps. According to a Human Rights Campaign study, queer white workers in the community made $0.97, Latinx workers made $0.90, Black workers made $0.80, Native American / Indigenous people made $0.70, and Asian / Asian Pacific Islanders (AAPI) made $1.00 for every dollar those outside of the queer community made. These numbers drop even lower when you look at the differences in gender identity. Across the same study of seven thousand people, researchers found men in the queer community were making $0.96, women were taking home $0.87, nonbinary folks and trans men were both making $0.70, and trans women were taking home $0.60 to every dollar made by someone outside of the LGBTQIA+ community.[22]

These pay discrepancies are felt even more when you think about the high cost of living to simply exist safely. Small cities and towns have their advantages, most notably that they are relatively inexpensive areas, but as a trade-off, racial, sexual, and gender diversity often suffer because of the smaller population. Oftentimes, people in queer communities feel safer knowing they will be accepted in places where they do not feel othered or like they're the only ones living there, which oftentimes are bigger cities with heftier price tags. As we discussed earlier, people don't want to feel tokenized or othered. Community and belonging are important to the human spirit.

Additionally, bigger cities tend to offer appropriate support for life happenings, such as medical care and treatment, event vendors, access to housing, job growth, fertility—the list goes on and on. Marriage laws giving rights to partners and families are imperative when attempting to financially exist or protect your future estate. A financial plan and money to execute it only helps.

A Note on Divorce and Prenups

It is commonly understood that one of the leading causes of divorce is money. Of course, there are a lot of unaddressed stressors that lead to divorce, and as we have learned, money is rarely about only the numbers. Whether it be a mismatch of priorities, overspending/underspending, or financial infidelity (the hiding, lying, or keeping secret of financial activities like racking up debt, hiding money, or lying about income), money is far too often a huge stressor for couples. Getting financially naked with your potential person is a must. It is shocking to me how many people would rather literally get naked than openly talk to their date about their salary, income, or debt. It is a wild demonstration of the fear associated with vulnerability. For as long as modern capitalism has been in effect, people have dealt with wealth disparity by pushing it into secrecy, positing that if it wasn't talked about, it didn't exist. For some, not being vulnerable to potential scams, criticism, or asks for money was a defense mechanism. For others, fear of being belittled, judged, or criticized prompted them to keep the financial aspects of their life private as a protective mechanism. Not wanting to be seen as unintelligent or weak for not knowing about personal finance has caused many people to clam up and never share what they are/were living through.

The financial impact of divorce can be devastating. Dasha Kennedy, also known as the Broke Black Girl, frequently shares the importance of not only being financially involved in the decisions made for the household and family but also financially independent just in case something changes in the relationship. While on the podcast *Brown Ambition* hosted by Tiffany Aliche and Mandi Woodruff-Santos, Kennedy strongly suggested female listeners "never take the backseat when it comes to finances because things can change in a heartbeat."[23] After getting divorced, she quickly realized that even though she and her ex-husband had not "officially" combined finances, she was reliant upon the second income to pay bills, ensure she had childcare, and maintain other supportive parts of their life. When they made the decision to separate, she was then put in the position of maintaining some of those bills with only her income. She noted, "We have to look at money as a gender-based issue when it comes to women. It is important that we know exactly what is going on because if things were to ever go left, we stand to lose more. That's another huge misconception about divorce—that women always walk away with the winning ticket."[24] Kennedy encourages her community to have more in-depth conversations about money and get honest with one another about how we were raised around money, knowing that our lived experiences in childhood will impact what happens with the money in our adult relationships. Sound familiar?

The importance of an emergency fund really shines during these instances. This is not to say that you need to hide money from your partner; you don't. But having some sort of cushion to take care of you and/or your family will be helpful should anything go awry. Journalist Lela Nargi wrote a *New York Times* piece titled "How to Rebuild Your Savings and Retirement After a Divorce" and highlighted that "divorced Americans are more likely than those who never experienced divorce to lack enough savings to retire at 65 with their accustomed quality of life." This factoid is further compounded when you adjust for "the brunt of the financial hit [being felt by women due to] both the expense of raising children and the negative consequences for their earnings of having child care and family responsibilities."[25] When you are going through a divorce, the last thing you should be worrying about is whether your basic needs are going to be met now and in the future. Regaining your financial footing after divorce is painful and time-consuming, and this affects many different experiences, from women who may have been told "they would be taken care of" to women whose retirement account was significantly reduced as an impact of the divorce.

It is hard to go into a partnership or marriage planning for the worst. I don't think anyone wants to believe their love will ever change, but sadly, sometimes it does. People change, tragedies happen, and love shifts all the time. Preparation helps lessen the devastation. In this way, prenups can help ensure both parties will be okay financially in the unfortunate event that things do not work out. Yup, we are going there, and no, prenups are not "just" for rich people. A prenuptial agreement, or prenup, outlines the financial standing of each party involved and lists how things will be divided in the event of a divorce. After potentially being married for some time, your financial standing might look different. I chatted with Maggie Johndrow, a certified divorce financial advisor, who shared, "Prenups are a useful tool for risk management. I find clients spend a lot of time thinking about, discussing, and planning on how to *build* wealth, but spend less time thinking of how to *protect* that wealth! A prenup is one of many tools that can help protect your wealth."

Prenups get a bad reputation, just like budgets. The stereotypical vision of a Charlotte York (yes, a *Sex and the City* reference) negotiating her prenuptial agreement to leave her with $1 million may seem less realistic when you're out of your mind in love at the beginning your marriage, but when considering your personal businesses or the unpaid labor of raising children, protecting your financial future is imperative. You just never know. Johndrow also told me that "when you're in engagement bliss, you likely don't want to be thinking of sad events—or you may think you're the exception to the rule, which can be dangerous thinking at times. Prenups have a bad reputation for the same reason life insurance does: No one likes to think about 'the bad,' whether that be getting a divorce or dying."

Speaking of death, preparation is also key when it comes to other types of tragic events like a sick, hurt, incapacitated, or recently deceased spouse. I know, none of us want to think about this happening, but not having access to accounts or knowing where the money is during a long-term medical event or in the case of death may place a horribly uncomfortable burden on you. Statistically, women tend to outlive men by four to six years, so it's helpful that we know what is going on in our financial lives, even if we are not the one managing it directly.[26] Clearly, there is a discrepancy here. Estate and will planning are just as important as retirement planning. I'm sure you've heard the horror stories of grieving families fighting over the potential inheritance from the will, or lack thereof, of a loved one. As with prenups, it is hard to think about events we don't want to happen anytime soon, but it's necessary to put a plan for your finances in place for when you or a loved one passes.

No matter what the composition of your partnership looks like, I want it to last as long as you want it to. I want nothing more than for you and your partner(s) to spend your lives together, basking in all things amazing. However, we do not always have control over what happens in our lives, and the unplanned and unimaginable happen far too frequently. Having a plan is necessary.

Money and Gender Roles

When my husband and I bought our house, the bank opened our mortgage account in his name. I know they had to have one of us on the account, but I was unsure why they automatically chose him and not both of us. Not only did I not like the optics of them putting his name on the account because he was a man, but also I was the one who managed the finances (more on that in a second), and to put it frankly, I was uncomfortable not having access to the account. In an effort to combat my discomfort, I made sure I was involved. No changes to the account could be made without coming to both of us. Although I manage our finances, I involve him at every step. We have a system, but to be honest with you, there is a part of me that is concerned that if anything happened to me, he wouldn't know where everything is.

It doesn't matter who takes on the majority of the financial management of the family as long as everyone knows what is going on. This level of communication extends to income brought into the family as well. More and more, women are becoming higher earners, and this is having a dramatic effect on marriages and dating (cis-hetero ones specifically). The cultural norms of men being the higher earners in relationships are now outdated. Toxic masculinity will tell you women shouldn't ever earn more. According to this sexist viewpoint, it is some sort of infraction on men for women to be more successful or make more money; our success makes them feel obsolete. Those who grow up believing this narrative have been failed by society. Men believing they are rendered useless if a woman is independent or financially independent says more about the harmful nature of attaching masculinity to net worth than it does about the inherent value men bring. While I detest patriarchy, I do believe men have a ton of value outside of bringing home the bacon. I have no time for patriarchy; it hurts all of us.

Sallie Krawcheck, cofounder and CEO of Ellevest, a robo-advisor investment platform, is notorious for saying in a

CNBC interview, "Nothing bad happens when women have more money," and that is the truth.[27] Money is unfortunately political, so we need to understand how we engage with it both individually and collectively. Then, we can be the change we want to see in the world and financially back that change.

I'm Not Good at Math

While we're on the topic of money and gender, I want to circle back to a limiting belief I've mentioned that is a close cousin to "If I don't look at it, it will go away." Much to the chagrin of STEM teachers everywhere, a common refrain we need to continue to chip away at is the misconception many girls and women have internalized: "I'm not good at math." I, too, felt like I was bad at math while growing up. I'd proclaim I didn't like it and throw a fit anytime I was expected to do it. Years later, however, when I was interning in a high school math classroom, I realized I did, in fact, enjoy math. Soon after, I began my personal finance journey and have found that I can crunch numbers quickly, and I enjoy the mental exercise of solving math problems. I'm glad I'm now in a place where math doesn't seem so foreign and mind-bending, but I acknowledge that many of us are not there yet. I understand. I held on to the mindset that math was not for me for so long, and the messages I received both implicitly and explicitly confirmed this thought process. Thank goodness I'm stubborn.

Before we get into the concrete steps of how to navigate your finances without the unfounded narrative of "If I don't look at it, it will go away" or "I am not good at math," we have to discuss two areas where we specifically keep our heads in the sand and, as a result, run the risk of leaving more money on the table: negotiating and investing. If you have a narrative that money and numbers are too difficult, then you likely won't find yourself at the negotiating table and you may have been told not to "worry your pretty little head" when it comes to any type of financial investment. I feel you. I was the same way, but times are different now, and it would benefit both you and your household if you accepted the challenge and committed yourself to learning these important topics.

Negotiating

Not having the opportunity to discuss or learn about money impacts all aspects of how you operate with it. It can feel much easier to let someone else handle it and dictate to you when you don't feel equipped to manage your own dollars. You'll be more apt to avoid any talk of salary or monetary discussions in the workplace and, as a result, stay as far away from negotiating as possible. After all, it's just easier. Right? This approach leaves many (mostly women) simply accepting the first offer and not asking for raises and further perpetuates a desire to keep their heads in the sand. Women leave upward of $1 to 1.6 million on the table as a result of not negotiating throughout their careers.[28] If that doesn't empower you, I don't know what will.

Although a casual million dollars is a life-changing amount of money, it is not about the money. It is about access and the potential impact. My friend Berna Anat, Financial Hype Woman and author of *Money Out Loud*, said, "Money is the language of survival in a capitalistic society."[29] Whether you are negotiating your wants and needs, advocating for benefits or a new salary, talking to your family, or negotiating a prenup, making sure you are financially comfortable and stable helps dissolve stressors for not only you but also those around you. If you were never taught how to feel stronger in using your voice, reach out to family and friends who can help or try to find online resources, like Mandi Woodruff-Santos's MandiMoney Makers community, that can help bolster that confidence within you. Networking with those you feel comfortable getting this level of support from will only help you in the long run. The rhetoric of "I'm just happy to be here" is how we have been conditioned to take what we are given and not put up a fuss about what we don't like or don't understand. This belief is harmful to not only us and our futures but also the futures of those who come after us. We got to this point through the efforts of our ancestors, and we, too, will be someone's ancestors, paving the way for our children decades down the road.

Investing

Beyond the longstanding systemic history that has put women and marginalized communities at a financial disadvantage, we must also consider the emotional impact that comes as a result. Believing that you are bad at math and there's nothing you can do about it will quite literally have you ignoring your money, reaching out to someone else to manage it, or costing you in the long run by not planning properly. People very commonly feel like they aren't in the market or investing because they aren't constantly checking their stocks and shouting "buy" or "sell" at their screens. The finance bro has corrupted the image of investing, coaxing us to believe that day trading is the only way someone can be good at investing or personal finance. This is but a small fraction of the reality of investing.

I want to say this very clearly: If you have money in the market—whether through individual stocks, bonds, an invested 401(k) or otherwise—you are investing! The image of a Patagonia vest over light-blue button-downs is but one image of finance. For most people, investing isn't exciting. It is long and slow and not filled with a ton of entertainment. If you ask me, that is how I prefer it. Set it and forget it. Investing is a commitment to your future self; you put your money in the market and see how it grows and compounds with time.

Now, contrary to what you may have been told, women outperform men on average in the stock market. The issue is that many women don't get into the market in the first place. Generally, some innate tendencies help us out when it comes to growing our money through investments. We tend to stick to plans longer, make less impulsive moves (blame it on the testosterone), and listen to the advice we are willing to ask for, among other things.[30]

Reflection Questions

- What type of role are you playing in your finances? Passive? Present? Aggressive?
- How much of the role you take with your finances has been influenced by societal expectations?
- What is holding you back from taking a more prominent or passive stance in your financial life?
- Do you feel comfortable talking about money with your partner? Why or why not?

More Than Relationships

As I mentioned in the opening of this chapter, we're focusing a lot on the role that gender plays in financial decisions, but I want to reiterate again that money avoidance is not only reserved for people in (cis-hetero) relationships! Before we close, I want to pivot a moment to acknowledge that there are a number of other situations where people put their head in the sand as a way of coping with their money narratives. One prime example is the business owner who wants nothing to do with their money. They don't look at their taxes, ignore their profit and loss statements (P&Ls), and hire someone else to handle the books. They may know the general direction of things, but they refuse to get into the numbers and, in fact, will do anything to avoid it.

In addition to all manner of entrepreneurs, I have been fascinated to find that so many people who work in finance feel that they do not know the necessary basics of what to do with their money, personally. Shocking! At the very least, shouldn't personal finance be included at some point during formal finance education? The answer is yes, but it has been overlooked for decades. The United States has only recently begun to integrate financial education into high school curriculums. Although this education isn't nationwide yet, there has been a push to introduce laws that combat the gap in financial education for youth. More school districts across the country are realizing the importance of financial education and are doing the work to bring it into the classroom more frequently so the next generation can avoid becoming the ostrich with its head in the sand and feel prepared to successfully manage their personal finances into adulthood. So when you find yourself feeling bad about how you should have known better, remember that the majority of people have no financial education whatsoever. It's about time for all of us to come face-to-face with our money, regardless of our relationship status, age, or current financial position.

Let's Get Financial: Lesson in Money

No matter your financial position, if you do not know what or where your money is, it is time to get financially naked with yourself. What do I mean by this? I want you to come face-to-face with your numbers and dive into what your financial life looks like in this present moment. Feel free to set a money date with yourself to go through everything in a calm setting. Eat your favorite food, set the mood, commit to remaining calm, and go in understanding that it could be triggering. If you are living with a partner or feel like your relationship could benefit from an open chat around finances, don't hesitate to include them as well. This level of self-awareness will benefit everyone involved.

First, get out a sheet of paper, an Excel document, or your favorite notes app. If you want something already set up for you, feel free to head over to my website (ajaevanscounseling.com) and download my guide. We are getting naked, baby!

1. Take several deep breaths to lower your heart rate and relax the nervous system.
2. On your paper or spreadsheet, make a header called Checking Accounts with two columns underneath it. Label the first column Institution; this is the name of the bank that houses your account. Label the second column Amount; this is the amount of money you have in that account (make sure you are putting this information somewhere safe).
3. Continue by listing all your checking accounts and the amount of money in each of them, and then when you're done, list the sum total of all of them at the bottom.
4. Now, repeat this for your savings accounts. On the back of the page or on a separate spreadsheet, create a new header called Savings Accounts with the same two columns and repeat steps 1 through 3 for all your savings accounts.

Bravo! Now, you are going to take similar steps for your debt. Remember to breathe!

1. First, create a header called Credit Cards and put three columns underneath it. Label the first column Institution, the second Amount, and the third Interest Rate. (This is the percentage rate of interest you are charged for that particular account. This can be different for each institution.)

2. Go through and list all your credit cards, the amounts charged on each, and the interest rate for each card. Feel free to put it into any order you'd like—random, smallest to largest amount, largest to smallest amount, or in order of interest rate.

3. List the sum total of all your charges at the bottom.

4. Now, do the same for any loans you may have (think car note, student debt, personal loan, mortgage, etc.). Repeat steps 1 through 3, but specifically for any loan amounts you have.

You're doing great! One last section to go: investments.

1. Create a header labeled Investments, and place two columns underneath it. Label the first column Institution and the second Amount.

2. Fill out this section with any money you have set aside for the future. This could include your 401(k) or 403(b) (a 401(k) for nonprofit employees), individual retirement account (IRA), Roth IRA, 529 plan (college savings account), or brokerage accounts (a type of investment account that allows you to buy and sell different types of investments). A little extra nugget of advice: Make sure your money is invested, not just sitting in the account waiting to be invested.

3. If you have any other accounts or money happenings that regularly come in and out of your life, feel free to list them as well. It's imperative that you keep tabs on how much money is coming into your household. (What's going out is important, too, but that is what your budget is for.)

Phew! You did it. How do you feel completing this audit? Did anything come up emotionally or financially that you were or were not expecting? Were you surprised by the amount of money you have in your checking, savings, or debt? Were you reminded of purchases or financial situations that you had worked to keep out of sight? Take note of all these emotions and thoughts in a journal.

Now, what do you do with this information? All this information will inform how you set your financial priorities and make your goals. Where do you want to be? Do you want more in your checking or savings accounts and less debt? Do you want to use your credit cards more wisely? Are there any loans you'd like to pay off sooner rather than later? What would make you feel the most comfortable financially? What do you want to change? Whether it's your debt, savings, retirement plan, or general financial awareness, it's always better to be aware and prepared than left in the dark. You got this!

Chapter 5

I Need the Fucking Pumpkins

The first few dips in temperature are making their appearance, casually reminding you that summer will soon be coming to a close. The chill was welcomed the second the calendar said September, but you rarely parade that factoid around to your sun-obsessed friends and family. While going about your usual Saturday morning routine, you realize you are almost down to your last roll of toilet paper. If the wild, wild west times of the COVID-19 pandemic taught you anything, it's that you should never get down to your last roll of toilet paper.

So, you add it to the small list of items you plan to get while out running errands today.

You pull into the oh-so-familiar parking lot and are immediately greeted with bright red lights in the shape of a bull's-eye, beckoning you in. After navigating several rogue carts and a few overly ambitious attempts to find parking close to the entrance, you settle on parking a little farther away. *I could use the walk*, you think.

Target isn't the only thing calling to you this morning. As the sliding doors open, you immediately realize that the in-house Starbucks has made a point to let you know your favorite fall companion is back in town; autumn lovers unite, the pumpkin spice latte is back. You get in line. *Fall is in the air, why not? Wait, does this make me basic? Do I care?*

"I'll have a grande pumpkin spice latte, please," you say with a smile. *Yup, this feels right.* As you walk away, you wrap your fingers around the cup, allowing the warmth to wash over you. Suddenly, you realize fall has descended upon the rest of the store as well. Out with the brightly colored bikini tops and water toys and in with the cardigans, blankets, and autumnal decor.

Damn, that sweater is cute.

Unbeknownst to you, the caffeine and sugar slowly start working their magic. With the smooth sounds of Arlo Parks playing in the background, the red-and-white signage begins to move you through the meticulously organized aisles. You decide right then and there, you will take your sweet-ass time roaming the aisles. You deserve it. Being alone with endless time to simply peruse is exactly what you need to feel . . . better? To feel . . . something. You relax into the familiar space, allowing your mind to clear and the stresses from the week to melt away. You quickly trade in your basket for a cart, just in case.

It all starts off so well intended, with not the toilet paper and dish soap you came for but rather the dollar spot hand towels printed with leaves and little bicycles. *These will look so cute in the kitchen*, you think as you sip and continue deeper into the store.

You find yourself grabbing shirts for your daughter. She obviously needs these because "fall fashion." Those little suede boots will go perfectly with this well-curated outfit; they make their way into the cart as well. You ignore the nagging feeling that your daughter will likely reject the boots, but the hope of your toddler's enthusiasm and love for her new earth-toned outfit blinds you. You quickly find yourself wondering if your son needs boots, too. *Wait, do I need boots? Everyone needs boots! It's fall, friends.*

You are feeling better already. *I deserve it*, you tell yourself (again), and you are right: You do. Before you know it, time seems to have stood still and your cart is full. Shocked, you begin to dig through what will soon be your latest haul: clothes, a water bottle, a new shade of lipstick or two, body wash, a book for your niece, something special for yourself, candles, and a whole lot of pumpkin decor. *Damn, I love fall.*

The promise of cozy nights in a clean living room gets me every time. Oh, and I need those pumpkins, too.

But you came here with a list and a budget. Your rational mind, the part of you that has some self-control and wants to say no, starts to betray you. The list on your phone and the cart you are pushing tell different stories. Your trip for necessary items has shifted to a self-care run to Target. *It can't be that much; I will just do a little self-edit of the cart.* You came for toilet paper and dish soap. *Shit. Have to be sure to get those.* You will eventually run out of body wash, so need to keep that. But what about these pumpkins? *It is fall. Won't the house look and smell so cute?* You envision your currently messy living room, magically cleaned without any effort from you, and your mantle filled with the pumpkins staring at you from inside your cart. That is how it *should* be. *Won't it feel good to come home to a tidy, clean, cozy, magazine-ready space that makes me want to curl up on the couch? It's decided.*

I NEED THE FUCKING PUMPKINS.

So, you get them, along with all those other things that weren't on your list.

Spoiler Alert: It's Not About the Pumpkins

This is a tale as old as time. It may not be pumpkins or even Target for you; it could be late-night Amazon shopping, shoes, books, stationery, or electronics. The item and location are unimportant. What I am referring to here is how quickly we can get swept up in the dopamine rush that is shopping.

Time for another neuroscience lesson, folks. Dopamine is considered our feel-good neurotransmitter. Our brilliant friends at Harvard Medical School said dopamine is "linked to love, pleasure, motivation and more, [its] signaling plays a central role in the brain's reward system. It is also critical for processes such as motor control, learning and memory."[31] No wonder shopping feels so good; our brain is literally telling us so. There has been a lot of discussion about what happens in our brains while we are shopping, but research continues to conclude that when it comes to shopping, the dopamine rush is coming from the anticipation of the purchase instead of the purchase itself.[32] You are excited by the browsing, thinking about the purchase. Like many things in our life, the anticipation is what hooks us.

You are not only contending with your emotions and relationship to money while walking the aisles or scrolling online. Marketing, my friends, is designed to do exactly what it does: silently suggest to you that you *need* these things. I am not naive enough to think our purchasing is the result of only our uninfluenced emotions. Marketing is designed to transport you from not spending to spending as quickly as possible. And damn, that shit is effective.

When I first learned that marketing is informed by psychology, I almost fell over. Sigmund Freud's (yes, *that* one) brother created the PR campaign that began championing capitalism to the public. Of course, it makes sense to understand human behavior when trying to sell, but in all honesty, I was shocked to learn how much it makes perfect sense. After all, what motivates people? Our emotions. Despite our consistent efforts to pretend we aren't emotional beings, humans love storytelling, connecting with people, feeling something. We crave it; it is just how we are built. To learn that the same principles and theories I pored over for years are used to influence people to spend their dollars was a revelation. There is a time and place to rail against marketing and the ills of extreme capitalism, some warranted and some not, but that is not what this book is about. However, its relevance is key to understanding how signifiers build on top of one another to prompt a purchase. The feelings we have during certain times of the year, like a change in season, are a perfect reason to market the importance of resetting or restocking.

That being said, let us go back to Target. What happened after you unexpectedly spent $375 at the checkout? To understand, we need to rewind and get honest about the thoughts and feelings that led to such a purchase. What was going on for you before you entered the store? When you sat in the car, what were you thinking? How were you feeling? Were you excited to be alone, happy for the break, relieved to be out of the house? All these things matter when we talk about our desire to purchase.

Real Life

While the Target scenario is true for many people, there are several ways a similar money issue might present itself. I recently started working with Michelle because she had had a harsh financial awakening. In a nutshell, a friend shared with Michelle that although she knew she should probably mind her own business, the friend could no longer stand by and watch Michelle make awful money choices and squander her funds. In asking Michelle what that meant, she told me she had never really paid attention to her money. She had a good job and was paid well, so she cycled through feast and famine. Michelle would live it up for a year or so, buying whatever she wanted, traveling wherever she wanted, treating friends and family, and footing the bill for group dinners and a host of other high-priced items. In the last year, she told me she had left the country four times and treated herself to pretty much every whim and desire she had. She was YOLO-ing hard.

The inquiry from her friend gave Michelle pause. She decided to get financially naked and look at her numbers. She did not like what she found. She had taken on a ton of extra debt through credit cards to fund her lifestyle. Looking at the magnitude of her cost of living, she felt completely overwhelmed about how she was going to pay it all back, so she reached out to me.

Our process started much like it does with any of my clients: learning about what their life had looked like up until that point. Through getting to know one another, with multiple layers of questions and a lot of tears, Michelle realized that in her adult life she was attempting to make up for being told no while growing up. She wanted to be able to show up for herself and everyone else as a loud, resounding yes. Even deeper than making up for all the times she heard no was her lack of self-esteem. She wondered what value she had to give if she wasn't financially giving to people. If she wasn't the fun yes that everyone wanted, who was she?

All the Feels: Target Edition

Sometimes I get to run errands alone, which is a big deal in my house, especially with two tiny humans running around shouting their every desire, thought, and feeling. During the height of the pandemic, going to run errands was usually the only way to shift out of my day-to-day routine. What I was looking for was a break, a moment to breathe, relief from the anxious feeling of not knowing what was going on in the world, of feeling trapped without so many things we used to enjoy. Errands were a welcomed change, Target in particular. I often joked with my husband that I went to Target to *feel something*. I did not know then that what I was searching for was to feel more like myself again, like I had autonomy and could let my thoughts wander without fear that I was dropping a responsibility to do so. I was a new mom and started my business full time the week New York City went into lockdown. The pressure was on.

Was I actually "finding myself" while roaming the aisles under those fluorescent lights? No, but I, too, convinced myself that I would work out more if I had a cute outfit or that cooking a meal every day would feel less tedious if I was doing so with a brand-new slow cooker. If I bought these totes for underbed storage, things in my house would always be clean. If I bought this KitchenAid stand mixer attachment, I would bake more. The cozy throw was the missing piece to my living room being "just right."

I would, we would, if only, when I buy . . . The wishful thinking goes on and on, and honestly, it does not end. What we are trying to do or say to ourselves is that we will be better on top of things, more this, less of that, different when and if we buy this. So many of us are simply relying on retail therapy and being *that* person to shift our mood and feel better. Instead of addressing what is going on emotionally, we resort to utilizing retail therapy in hopes that the temporary relief will dissolve the real issue(s). That temporary relief, by the way, is due in part to the dopamine rush we experience in anticipation of our purchase. The excitement of the purchase is fun and can be great, but it is only a Band-Aid when we use it to cope with heavy feelings we are leaving unaddressed.

What's the "Why"?

So, what is really going on when you feel the need for retail therapy or find yourself aimlessly putting items in your cart, literally or virtually? Are you spending your money when you feel bad about something else? What are you trying to feel better about? What truth are you running from, masking, or ignoring? Shall we name it and give your bank account a rest?

Spending money is a huge coping strategy for a lot of us. Honestly, capitalism requires it. People use work, sex, drinking, exercise, and a whole slew of other things to help them deal with the realities of life. Money is no different. This is why marketing is so effective; we have been fed the story that one purchase is truly going to make us feel better. Honestly, sometimes it does (which is also okay). Unfortunately, the one-purchase fallacy is really just the dopamine doing its job. For me, during the height of the COVID-19 pandemic, it was less about what I wanted to feel and more about what I was avoiding. What I did *not* want to feel was bored, worried, stifled, or confused about integrating my new identities. Like many people, my usual coping strategies, like hanging out with friends, going on date nights, or walking around New York City, were cut off. Spending money while on a rare errand run was a new escape from the everyday realities.

It is important to make the distinction between coping and distraction. A coping skill or strategy (I will use these terms interchangeably) is an activity done to help healthily alleviate an unpleasant feeling. Distraction, on the other hand, is when you do something to take you away from a situation or thought. Here is the tricky part: Distraction can be used as a coping skill at times. It is not a permanent solution to the problem, but it can help when you're trying to manage discomfort. Eventually, though, you will need to stop distracting yourself, sit with your uncomfortable, raw feelings, and slowly learn how to name, validate, feel, and move through those feelings. Michelle, for example, had to come to grips with being told no when she was younger and realizing her value was greater than what she paid for.

Trauma of Money (TOM), which we talked about earlier, emphasizes the importance of allowing our emotional energy to move through us, stating that "when energy isn't discharged, it gets stuck in the body." Remember when I told you that unaddressed trauma lives in our body (see chapter 2) long after the triggering incident? This is why thoroughly processing our emotional discomfort is essential for effectively managing our feelings of stress, discomfort, and anxiety. Coping with your feelings through spending and/or shopping can give you a false sense of relief, but a dopamine hit is masking how you truly feel. No real resolution to the problem or your feelings has come; it's just been hidden.[33] When we're stressed or activated, our bodies go through a four-stage stress cycle:

1. **Activation.** This is when a trigger occurs, whether it be a thought, memory, smell, or observation.

Your body is now alert to the stressor, no matter the location of the threat, whether internal or external. Sometimes you may not know the trigger, but your body will start the cycle regardless. This is often seen in people who have lived through traumatic events. Your body starts producing more cortisol and adrenaline spikes to help prepare the body to respond.

2. **Mobilization.** Your mind and body are taking in information to decide what is needed to maintain safety and respond to the stressor. This stage is commonly referred to as fight, flight, or freeze—your heart rate changes and nonessential systems slow to allow for quick response.

3. **Deactivation.** In this stage, you begin to cope with the impact of the stressor, allowing your body to return to homeostasis and a resting state.

4. **Rest.** You and your body are in a neutral state. There is no longer an emotional or physical trigger.

The problem with the way we often deal with stress is that we are not completing the stress cycle. We bury the feeling with maladaptive coping skills, like scrolling, shopping, or distracting ourselves in hope that the stressor goes away. Particularly with money, this leaves us in a chronic state of activation and stress, leading to an array of mental and physical challenges, including irritable bowel syndrome, high blood pressure, heart disease, troubled sleep, muscle aches, pain, and a slew of other potentially dangerous issues.[34] Humans are not meant to hold their stress in this way.

Here are a few proven ways you can effectively move through the stress cycle, so you aren't walking around with a chronically activated system:

- Exercise in a way that feels good to you
- Deep, intentional breaths
- Talk it out
- Laugh or cry
- Engage in a creative outlet
- Be affectionate with another person or pet[35]

Reflection Questions

- Reflect on a time you spent impulsively to distract from or cope with a negative feeling.
- How did you feel right before the purchase? How did you feel afterward?

- Upon your reflection, do you see a pattern in using money to cope with uncomfortable feelings?
- Are there other ways you have started working on the root of your negative feelings?

Now It Is Time for Action

So, how does needing the pumpkins at Target show up in your finances? I mean, I think we can all answer that quickly: You see your receipts. I know I am not alone in saying that Target *blows up* my budget (and, yes, Target is a line item for me). I will spend countless hours scrolling through all the beautifully curated Pinterest accounts feeling like if I could just find the right plant, I will be able to fulfill the perfect mix of Scandi-industrial, Afro-cool chicness. (That's a thing, right?)

Of course, rationally, I know that scrolling and aimlessly making purchases to capture a "vibe" will not get me closer to my financial goals. However, we are all on this journey of reckoning with our money and the emotions it brings up. And we *know* one thing about emotions: They aren't always rational.

Let's Get Financial: Lesson in Money

As we learned in the last chapter, it's important we get financially naked so we can get real about our money and take an honest look at the state of our finances. You can't change what you don't know is a problem, so coming to terms with where you are financially helps define your priorities. Sometimes, realizing how much you are spending helps start the process of shifting your behavior, which involves realizing what you are doing, acknowledging what works and what doesn't, what you want to be different, and how to work toward shifting your habits. Humans are creatures of habit, and when it comes to money, our habitual behavior can rule us, causing us to mindlessly save or spend whenever we experience activating circumstances. (You might be thinking, is *saving* mindlessly actually a bad thing? I will tell you more about that a bit later.)

Although I want you to feel better about your money, I want you to understand yourself more. Now that you've revealed your spending numbers by getting financially naked, take a moment in your journal to decide what you want your life to look like financially, professionally, personally, socially, mentally, and spiritually. How do you want to feel? Give yourself a moment to imagine what it would be like to cultivate the happiest, most stable life you can imagine. Let that be your guide in creating your goals.

Then, you can create a plan to execute. The entirety of your financial life will not be determined by the dreaded b-word, but we do have to look at it, even if briefly. Having and creating a budget gets such a bad reputation, with many people feeling like they're going to be restricted and told no, but I don't look at it this way. I think of a budget as a way to understand what our open boundaries are. You have to be real with yourself about what you actually spend and how you can make a shift without it feeling so extreme that you don't stick to it. I honestly could not care less what you call it—a spending plan, a budget, a "killing it" plan (like my family calls it)—but having a general idea about what your monthly spending looks like is a must. Understanding what it costs to run your home and live your life allows you to effectively plan for your future and enjoy your money as you work toward those goals.

With that, be sure there is room to spend on fun things you love and enjoy. For some, it may be the custom latte or avocado toast people just seem to love to hate on millennials for enjoying. You can strive to have all things with a budget. This is why it is important to be honest about what you want and where your priorities are, so you can build it into your plan.

Create a line item to include the things that bring you joy, like eating out, traveling, or decorating your home. Knowing you are going to spend on those things helps you feel more comfortable and capable of sticking to your budget. Of course, you have to make sure your basic needs are covered before you add any extras. You may not be able to spend as much as you would like on the fun things, but it's important to include small joys along the way. Can you imagine? No guilt, no buyer's remorse! After all, you already carved out space for it. Many of us convince ourselves that we deserve things when we want something, and you would be right. You do deserve it. But what you deserve and what you can afford have nothing to do with each other. They are two totally separate things. The sooner we separate the value we see in ourselves from what we can afford, the happier we will be. Free yourself with your budget. It doesn't have to be restrictive.

When it comes to making a budget, there are a few different schools of thought you can follow, so it's important to keep in mind that personal finance is personal. Do what works for you. The following is by no means exhaustive, but here are a few of the most popular methods. Feel free to mix and match and switch things up as your circumstances and comfort level change.

50/30/20 rule. This was designed to give people an example of how to live a more financially balanced life. It is set up by calculating your total income after taxes and breaking it down into three buckets: 50 percent for needs (think housing, food, transportation to and from work, utilities, etc.), 30 percent for wants and entertainment (think Netflix, takeout, dinner with friends, hobbies, etc.), and the last 20 percent for saving and paying off debt.

Cash envelope system. With this system, you'll break down different categories of your monthly spending—say, housing costs, groceries, phone, coffee . . . whatever you decide are the categories you put your money toward each month to live. You'll then label each envelope with a category and fill each one with the amount of money you intend to spend on it. You only have the money in each envelope, and when it is gone, it's gone. No further spending unless you are taking from another category.[36]

Digital envelope system. This system is exactly like the cash envelope system, except you are using different digital accounts, or buckets within an account, to represent each category instead of cash.

Zero-based budgeting. This system requires you to start from zero each month, allocating all your income to different categories of spending with the goal of giving every single dollar you earn a purpose or job. With this system, you know what and where each dollar of your income will be going before it lands in your account.

The interesting part of all these methods is that you can utilize more than one for your budgeting system. For example, you might practice the 50/30/20 rule, but take those amounts and stuff cash envelopes. As I mentioned before, there are a multitude of methods available to budget well, even beyond what I've shared here. There's pen and paper, apps, spreadsheets—the possibilities are endless. You may be wondering which is the best to use, and I often give the same answer whenever I am asked this by my clients. The best system is the one you will use. You can spend all the money or no money on creating a budgeting system, but if you don't use it, it is useless. Simple is always easiest to start quickly, but finding a system that works for your lifestyle is paramount.

So, What Now?

The whole habit-loving gang, James Clear of *Atomic Habits* fame included, has written extensively about how habits cannot be broken, only shifted. So, you already know it's going to take some work for you to make the changes you want with your money. A lot of my clients mistakenly feel like once they uncover their money problem(s), they are healed, cured even. Unfortunately, that is rarely the case. The real work begins when you have to start making different decisions that go against your instinct to do what you have always been doing. You may have been operating the old way for decades, so give yourself grace when making a change. This type of shift takes time. You are going to mess up. It is okay because it is part of the process. Treat each hurdle as a learning experience.

And, finally, you may be wondering if or when you need to make a change. First, stop to notice whether there is a pattern in how you are feeling. Are you complaining about the same things over and over? Do you feel like you knew better but kept "messing up"? Are you struggling to stick to your budget? Next time, before falling prey to your normal spending habits, pause before you spend and check in with yourself. You can do so in the following ways:

Emotionally. Be aware of whether you're spending to cope with or bury a feeling. Double-check that you are balanced or feeling neutral. Ask yourself if you are HALT: hungry, angry, lonely, or tired.[37] Ensure that you are spending because you want to and can afford to, not solely because you're upset. If you find that you are spending to get out of a negative mood, try to take care of your needs first by utilizing one of the techniques to complete the stress cycle. After you do that, if you find yourself wanting to spend the money, that is okay. This exercise is more about learning how to healthily cope with your feelings before you spend money. I want you to enjoy your money, but not solely because you are trying to feel better.

Financially. Go buy the fucking pumpkins! I want you to enjoy your money just as much as you put it toward your goals. If it brings you joy, do it, but first take some time to realize why you may be craving that joy in the first place. And don't forget to check with your budget. Future you deserves just as much financial wellness and stability as the current version of you.

Reflection Questions

- Are you aware of how you feel before you go shopping?
- How often do you find yourself wanting to shop when you are upset?
- When do you find yourself craving or looking forward to spending money?
- How do you cope with your feelings when you are upset?
- What are three alternative things you can do outside of spending money to help you change your mood?

Chapter 6

Keeping Up with the Joneses

Havve you ever found yourself perusing photos of your second-grade classmate going on yet another vacation? You haven't spoken to them in decades, but you can't help wondering whether their "perfect" life is really all that perfect. Have you ever stared at your closet, thinking you have no "good" clothes because you saw whoever with the latest fit? Maybe it was a friend of a friend you barely know, but you obviously can't unfollow them because that would be rude. Every day in real life and on social media, people are out here looking like they are living their best fucking life, going to dinners, hanging with friends, and traveling the world while you feel exhausted from ordinary demands, most definitely not feeling fabulous. You ask yourself over and over: *How can they afford that?* And then the sneaky follow-up question comes in: *Why can't I afford that?* It is easy for your mind and emotions to tell you a different story from what's real, especially with the carefully tailored facades that are so often perpetuated online. To keep up, we can quickly ignore what is in our bank account and all our financial priorities in lieu of what feels or looks good. But our financial boundaries and priorities set the tone for what is possible for us and what isn't, so it's important we spend some time setting these for our long-term success. As a result, this chapter is all about the fancy-ass Joneses that we love to hate and the ways we can resist trying to keep up with them.

Who Are the Joneses Anyway?

There are a couple of origins of the phrase "keeping up with the Joneses." One is from a prominent wealthy family in the late 1800s and early 1900s who built large estates in and around New York City. The second comes from the humbler beginnings of a 1913 comic created by Arthur R. "Pop" Momand. The comic, which ran until the 1940s, highlighted the ups and downs of the McGinis family as they attempted to climb the social ladder and keep up with their neighbors. Their neighbors, the Joneses, were never seen but often referred to, cementing the last name as the metaphorical way of referring to neighbors, especially without naming who or what you are attempting to keep up with.[38]

Despite its origins over a century ago, the phrase is still a mainstay in how we observe and verbalize comparisons. Today, the Joneses are not only your neighbors or the latest "it" family; they are the standard we compare our everyday activities to. Bachelorette trips, birthday celebrations, and even dinners have all become competition and comparison's playground.

I, obviously, can't talk about the Joneses without talking about the most Jonesy family of our generation. The Kardashian family burst onto the scene in connection to the O. J. Simpson trial, Kim's sex tape, and then with the biggest splash of all, their record-breaking reality show, *Keeping Up with the Kardashians*. You can say whatever you want about the family, but their influence on pop culture—the good, bad, and ugly—has and will continue to be lasting. They took the concept of reality TV a step further, removing the protective walls from celebrity culture and letting the world see their most intimate, drama-filled moments. They were the queens of social media, branching "reality" into the realm of influencer.

Social media gave way to a whole new level of availability, thus deepening how and what we are able to compare. We no longer wondered what the Joneses were up to; we could see it in a well-edited highlight reel. I am sure this is why reality shows like *Keeping Up with the Kardashians* and influencer culture continue to be so popular today.

You often hear that social media isn't real. When you are scrolling and see the same face posting several times a day, it can be hard to believe that you aren't seeing the majority of a person's life. But it is true that you are seeing a lot and nothing, all at the same time. A thirty-second clip of someone's day shows you exactly what they want you to see: them getting ready, getting to their destination, having the best time, and potentially settling in after they have gotten home. What you don't always see is the unfolded laundry that is driving them crazy, the canceled babysitter and scramble to find childcare, or the "I am not going to make it" text they had to send their bestie yet again because they were too busy working. It's a totally curated showcase of life someone can design and present. Some go out of their way to be more real, but no one wants to put every detail of their messiness out there for the world to see. Strangers tend to not be very nice, and people often have a lot of opinions they aren't afraid to share from behind the safety of their keyboard.

This is why it's not helpful to compare your life as you sit in your sweats and finish a bowl of ice cream to the images you swipe past. No matter what it seems like is going on for them on the outside, the inside can look completely different—and vice versa! I am going to let you in on a little secret: Everyone's got problems. Big, small, manageable, or unmanageable, nothing is perfect. You can be rich and miserable or broke and the happiest person in the world. With social media, the voyeurism of being able to see what other people are doing has truly been all the marketing anyone would need. There is a reason marketing has evolved with social media. It works because that is where people are. Influencers and content creation have provided a direct line into the homes—and hands—of potential customers with perfectly curated outfits, vacations, homes, and household items for you to judge or compare yourself against. Before you know it, a new version of Carrie Bradshaw's voice is ringing in your ears saying, "I couldn't help but wonder, am I just broke or am I broken?" Well, I hate to ruin it for you, but Carrie Bradshaw was both fabulous and definitely broke. And honestly, sometimes she was broken. Life is hard, and no matter who you are, what you have in the bank, or what you show on social media, sometimes life beats you up.

All the Feels: The Comparison Game

You would be hard-pressed to find anyone who has not at least thought about how their life measures up to someone else's. Keeping up with the Joneses for me was watching my neighbors bring home a new car and thinking, *I want a new car.* Clearly, I was suffering from immediate onset amnesia because my reality quickly retorted, *Bitch, you* do *have a new car!* My less than two-year-old SUV (that I deemed necessary for two kids and a fifty-pound goldendoodle) was parked right next to me. My temporary amnesia took over before I had an opportunity to check it. I conveniently forgot about the realities of my life the second I saw someone else's hot new toy. *That* is what keeping up with the Joneses will get you. How quickly we forget that we might be the Joneses to someone else.

Here's the thing, though: Comparing yourself to those around you doesn't have to be a bad thing. The insidiousness of it begins to blossom if and when your negative voice starts to spew bullshit about yourself upon seeing someone else leveling up. It is wild and powerful. I literally talk about these thoughts and actions all the time, and when I'm not talking about it with clients, I am usually researching or reading about it, and even then, I sometimes succumb to the draw. Is this consumerist capitalism at its finest? Or perhaps my old money narratives and beliefs are creeping back in to slap the sense out of me? I'm still not always sure.

So, what is the deal? It is easy to believe keeping up happens in a bubble, but we know it doesn't. I watch my neighbors, literally and figuratively, bust their asses working and showing up for their families, yet I still feel that somehow I won't get to experience the ease and poise of how they operate, even when I know everyone struggles (parenting ain't easy, kids). That is just it; the Joneses are everyone and no one. We frequently believe that everyone else has it together, that they somehow are doing everything right, but we also somehow believe we are simply wrong . . . in every sense of the word. I know it isn't always as doom and gloom as I'm making it sound, but I have had the honor of sitting with twenty- to forty-somethings who feel like they haven't quite gotten the hang of adulting. There is this overwhelming sense that they missed a set of directions to life. But the mere fact that we desire to see, hear, or watch the lives of others lets us know that other people feel the same way we do, perhaps are even just as confused, too. I promise you are not the only one.

For someone out there, *I* am the Joneses. I'm not naive to think my suburban life outside of New York City isn't something someone is wishing for. Shit, I was hoping and wishing for it at some point, and now that I am here, let me tell you, maintaining it isn't easy. Outside of the work my husband and I have done to get here, there are privileges that allow us to stay. A lot of people think financial privilege is only about generational wealth, and although that is one form, other privileges—like education, sponsorship, opportunities, job advancement, salary, and location—help immensely.

According to a 2023 article published by Indeed, the average national salary in the United States is $55,640.[39] It can be extremely challenging to survive, live, and thrive on that salary while having a family, living in an expensive city, and trying to fight off capitalism's endless appetite for consumption of all kinds. Lifestyle creep, the gradual increase in spending as your income goes up, definitely plays a role, and so does keeping up with the Joneses. Comparison and spending to keep up will have you spending money you do not have. Have you ever been in a situation where you know you can't quite afford some of the extras you want? Things that you see others seemingly enjoying effortlessly, like dinners, trips, a new place, clothes? The thought of not being able to afford one of those purchases makes you question yourself. Negative thoughts start creeping in about the value you bring if you can't afford something, if you are "less than" or don't have your shit "together" because you don't have the money. Feeling like we can't or won't get what we want, especially if what we want makes us feel better about ourselves, has a way of corroding our self-worth and mental health, and before we know it, we are swiping our credit card telling ourselves, *I'll will worry about it later.* This is why it's imperative we get in front of our desire to keep up with others by filling in the gaps caused by living expenses, needs, and wants.

So, how do we do this? I'll tell you: debt.

What Is Debt?

Simply put, debt is an amount of money owed or to be paid back to a lender. It typically comes in the form of a line of credit (credit cards or a loan, such as a mortgage or car note), but it may also be a bill from an institution, as in the case of medical debt. Despite the multitude of opinions about debt, people go into debt for a variety of reasons. While keeping up with the Joneses may be one reason, it most definitely isn't the only one. So, what exactly is debt and how does it affect us personally? There are a few important terms you should know that may be connected to debt.

Your **interest rate** is the percentage you are charged on top of the amount of money or credit you were billed or loaned. You may also see it called **annual percentage rate (APR)**. This is generally what makes debt so tough to pay back because it adds extra money on top of the original balance you owe. For example, let's say you are approved for a credit card with a 15 percent interest rate. (Be aware that credit card interest rates today are typically between 18 percent and 24.99 percent, so read the fine print, folks.) If you have not paid off your balance by the end of your billing cycle, which is usually twenty-eight to thirty-one days long, the financial institution or lender will charge you 15 percent of any remaining balance on top of the balance itself.

This is where compound interest comes in; it can either be your best friend or your worst enemy, depending on what account it's attached to. **Compound interest** is the concept that your interest grows over time. Staying with the credit card example, let's say you have a $100 charge that you did not pay off at the end of the month. At 15 percent interest, you would be charged an additional $15 on top of the $100 you already owe. Now, let's say you only pay your minimum payment of $10, so your credit card balance is now $105. On your next bill, you will be charged interest on the $105, not the original $100. What some people don't know is that credit card interest typically compounds on a daily basis. This is why it's important to pay more than your minimum payment as often as possible to keep your balance low.

Compound interest grows quickly and can end up costing you money, even when you aren't actively using your card. As an added piece of caution, be careful of using the entirety of your credit balance. If you max out your card, the interest that is applied will push you over your card limit, and you best believe there are fees associated with that, from a hike in your interest rate to a late fee, or even a lower credit limit.

I know that is a lot of doom and gloom, but it doesn't have to be all bad. Some people have figured out how to utilize credit cards for all the perks and benefits and avoid their pitfalls. Folks who do this have researched and planned and are able to execute the discipline required to use credit cards sparingly and pay off their balance before too much interest occurs. As I mentioned before, compound interest can also be your best friend and help you grow your wealth, but we will get to that a bit later.

What Is "Good" Debt?

There are a lot of opinions about what constitutes "good" or "bad" debt. I have mixed feelings about these kinds of labels, but for the sake of explanation, I'll use these terms. Bad debt is typically looked at as **high-interest debt**, which is considered anything with an interest rate of 7 percent or above. If you are wondering why it's 7 percent, it is because the average rate of return people earn on their invested money is around 7 to

9 percent. In short, you would make more money investing rather than rushing to pay off your good debt. Regardless, bad debt is typically the hardest for people to get out of because of the high rate of compounding interest.

The issue I have with these labels is that when wealthy people utilize debt, it is looked at as them leveraging their net worth to purchase assets that will eventually make them more money. But if non-wealthy people utilize debt, it is often frowned upon. I am not down with the verbiage of a tool being highlighted as a positive or negative to further stigmatize people. For many, especially people of color, debt allows for access to things we wouldn't have been able to afford without it. I know I would have never been able to afford graduate school if I didn't take out student loans, and for some people, taking out a small personal loan to get a car or open a business is necessary for security and peace of mind. What I will say, though, is there are debts that are going to cost you more than others, so it's wise to be aware of what you're getting into.

In all honesty, as important as the numbers are, I am more concerned about your feelings regarding the debt you have. As we've discussed, debt can be extremely expensive, and while I want you to have all the things your heart desires, including clothing, a nice home, and a reliable car, to name a few examples, I don't want you to sacrifice your mental health or future to pay for things of the past—and definitely not because you were trying to keep up with the damn Joneses.

Debt can make people feel shame, guilt, and anxiety, which can quickly spiral into despair, sadness, and depression. I have no time for that, and I certainly don't want this for you. Once I realized how shitty people felt, I made it my mission to help people move through their personal finance goals with self-compassion. While dealing with debt can be incredibly emotional, there are ways to lessen its impact on your life and wallet. We'll get into some of these tips and tricks later in the chapter.

The Debt Trap

Saprina of Saprina Talks Money shared via TikTok, "We look at other people around us and they look successful, but I am here to tell you that most people are in debt." We quickly assume other people are doing far better than we are because they look like they are living the dream, they look successful, but she's right, "the Joneses are in debt."[40] As of March 2023, Americans held $17.05 trillion worth of household (mortgages) and non-housing (auto, student, credit card, other [ahem . . . medical]) debt.[41] Ali and Josh Lupo of the FI Couple shared on Instagram, "The 'American Dream' is a debt trap," citing the high cost of college, weddings, homes, and cars as a way "we trap people in their 20s" and watch as "they spend the next 35+ years giving most of their time to a job to pay it all off."[42] Ouch! That one touched a nerve. I still have student loan debt and definitely paid tens of thousands of dollars for my wedding. I loved it and very much do not regret it, but that is me.

As with financial matters, debt included, this all goes back to your money narrative. At any point in your life have you felt like you weren't good enough if you didn't have [insert item here]? The answer far too often is yes, especially when we're younger. As we learned in the last chapter, when we're stressed out, feeling bad about ourselves, triggered, or upset, it is easy to interrupt the stress cycle with the empty promises of retail therapy. Damn, that dopamine rush is strong, and it feels good. It takes a hell of a lot less time, therapy, and intro-spection to soothe our emotions with purchases than it does to do the deeper work. Growing, healing, and moving on is hard, and so is becoming a person who sees and moves in the world differently. This shift can be especially difficult when others aren't prepared for your shift. Remember those crabs in the barrel from chapter 2?

Picture This

A client's engineer friend planned and booked a trip to Paris with her mom without discussing the finances first. Mom thought her daughter could afford the trip outright, so she didn't mention it, but her daughter neither communicated nor had the heart to tell her mom that money was tight, so she got a second job to pay for it. While I respect her dedication to her mom and the determination to make it happen, she was doing too much. Still, there's no need for her to feel bad about the debt she has accrued. It is what it is. All she can do is move forward with the proper tools to remedy the situation and avoid making the same choice in the future.

Debt in itself is neutral, but people have created a culture around having debt as some kind of moral failing for certain people. Money, debt, and numbers have no emotion, but people most certainly do. Society has decided who gets to have debt and who doesn't, and it has painted some damning narratives about what it means for someone to carry debt with sayings like "You are irresponsible," "You should have known better," "You make so much money, I can't believe you are in debt," and "You are bad with money if you have debt." These ideas do nothing but shame people, which we've learned breeds isolation and can quickly lead to poor self-esteem and depression if left unchecked and unaddressed. That is not how we are trying to live, but it is a real aspect of how people feel and live when struggling with money or debt.

When you start to dive into how you feel about your debt, financial anxiety can begin to rear its ugly head, causing persistent concern and worry about your money that interrupts your ability to function. I introduced the concept of financial avoidance in chapter 4, and I want to take a moment to revisit it here because of the role avoidance plays when it comes to financial anxiety specifically related to debt. You may find that you completely avoid your bills, struggle to start the process of managing your finances, lose sleep, become flustered or agitated at the thought of money, or struggle to move past the debilitating wall between wanting to move on but not being able to. Phew, it's so much. A client shared, "I would lie awake in bed thinking about my debt. Thinking how I could kick the financial can down the road a little longer. I could feel the tightening in my chest, my palms getting sweaty, and my heart racing. I was losing my fucking mind. I knew I was just in debt, but I wanted to live the way I wanted to, the way I felt I deserved to, but I couldn't afford it. Getting takeout here or there isn't so bad, we weren't buying clothes all the time. I felt like a failure. How was it possible I built this life but couldn't afford it? Looking at the family I love so much, wondering how I let it get this bad."

When you are financially anxious, you might avoid your money. Avoiding negotiating when you know you could and should, casually putting off necessary financial maintenance, ignoring your incoming bills, and lastly, potentially pushing money away. I know, I know, you are probably like "What? Who would ever?" A lot of times it doesn't look as cut-and-dried as saying no to money. Usually, it's more complex, like not negotiating for a higher salary when you know you aren't at market rate or not sending invoices for work rendered because the thought is overwhelming. All of this is done because you believe deep down that money is bad or that people with money are bad. You don't want to be associated with that, so you push it away and avoid it in an attempt to not be seen as bad, too. But this only sabotages your financial success because of what you think it means if you have money.

Let's Get Financial: Lesson in Money

The concept of keeping up with the Joneses is the perfect example of just how much a lack of financial education and an unwillingness to inspect your money emotions can tank your finances. Without realizing it, you might be unnecessarily spinning your financial wheels, suffering from lifestyle creep, and ending up in deeper debt. While making "good" or enough money is fantastic, I don't want you to assume that it will fix all your problems or even encourage healthier spending habits. Money can fix a lot of things, but you can't outearn bad habits, emotional baggage, or lack of information. Flexing and looking rich will have you broke while making multiple six figures. No, thank you. On the flip side, I've had clients who do all the right things with their money yet still feel shitty about their relationship with money. This goes to show that it isn't always about how much money you have but how you feel about it.

Remember twenty-something Aja? I thought I could keep up with my friends because I was making more money when I moved to New York City, but in reality, I was draining my accounts and going into debt. I was not living my best life, even though my social life was banging. I was stressed the hell out, and I got good at relieving my money stress by, you guessed it, spending more money. I did not have goals, I didn't know how money worked, and it was quite literally costing me.

I want more for you, for me, for all of us. I want you to learn from my mistakes and understand not only how money can work for you but also how you can spend on the things you want and need without messing with your future plans and goals. As I mentioned before, there are a few ways you can lessen the impact of your debt, so let's dive in and start untangling some of these methods.

Debt Payoff Methods

Unfortunately, when it comes to getting out of debt, you need a strategy; you cannot willy-nilly this and throw your money all over the place because you are overwhelmed and want to feel better soon. The length of this process can be a major hang-up for people because, most times, people never see or feel like they are making any progress. The intention is there, but it can lack direction, leaving them confused and in the same position they started in.

Now, before you pick one of the strategies I outline here, if possible, *stop* using your credit cards or any other revolving credit line. You can't dig yourself out of debt while simultaneously adding to it. Sometimes this can't be avoided, so if that is the case for you, make sure your debt paydown shovel is bigger than whatever you are adding to it monthly.

Next, you need to know your numbers! I know it is hard to wrap your head around these kinds of details, but you know what else is hard? Not living your best life because too much of your money is going to debt. Paying off debt may not be a priority for everyone; it can feel like a never-ending climb, but if you are ready to make debt payoff one of your priorities, consider me your cheerleader. I believe in you! It may be grueling, but it is possible.

The personal finance community often says you have two options when it comes to your budget and paying off debt: You can either cut your expenses or make more money. Keep this in mind as you consider the following strategies to supercharge your payoff plan. Remember the work you did earlier in the book getting financially naked and making a budget? It is coming in handy now. When you know your numbers and have room in your budget to include things that bring you joy, you are able to funnel extra money toward your debt or other financial priorities. Not to mention staying on your debt pay-off journey will be easier because you will not burn yourself out as quickly by sacrificing everything you enjoy for the sake of paying off your debt. I am here for balance and a realistic outlook on living that leaves space for you to accomplish your goals and feel good while you do it.

Before you start paying off debt, it is best to have something saved for emergencies. Whether it is a couple of thousand dollars, the recommended three to six months' worth of income, or some other amount, having enough money saved to cover your household should anything come up during your payoff journey will ensure that you don't go back into debt.

Okay, so let's get started! The first step before you pick a debt payoff strategy is to list all the debts you are interested in paying off during this journey. Your list can include credit cards, student loans, car loans, outstanding bills, your mortgage, literally any and everything; it is up to you. Don't forget to include the name of the institution, amount owed, minimum monthly payment, and interest rate. Now that that's done, let's get into these strategies. Like anything else involving finances, the best method is the one that works for you, so take your time choosing the one that will fit best into your lifestyle.

With the **debt avalanche** method, organize the list of debt you already created in order of highest interest rate to lowest. Then, as you pay the minimum on all debts each month, throw any and all of your extra money toward the highest interest rate first. Continue to do this until that first highest interest debt is paid off, then use your extra money to pay off the next highest interest rate. Continue this method until all debts have been paid off. With this method, you will start strong like an avalanche and conquer your debts with momentum from the beginning, knocking out the accounts that have the highest potential to hold you back first. People love this method because you end up paying less in interest over time, which helps you save money in the long run.

The **debt snowball** is the opposite in a way: Organize your list of debt from lowest-owed amount to highest. Like the debt avalanche, continue making the minimum payments on all your debts, but throw your extra money to the lowest total amount. Once that's paid off, roll those extra funds over to the next lowest amount owed. This method ramps up motivation quickly by getting you a win as soon as possible. Like a snow-ball, the more you get it going, the faster it picks up the pace, getting bigger and bigger.

While less popular, the **emotional method** can be moti-vating for some people. This method focuses on paying off the one debt that annoys you the most. Financial experts often advise against approaching your money with emotions first, but as you can tell, I am flipping that notion on its head. People have feelings, and when we ignore them, they come back to bite us in the ass. This method may have you paying a bit more in the long run or not optimizing the numbers to the max, but it isn't about that. It is about getting rid of that one debt you hate for whatever reason. As always, continue making your minimum payments on everything else and throw all your extra money at this one debt. From there, you can continue paying off debt in the order of annoyance or feel free to start utilizing a different method.

Other methods I have seen involve paying off the debt with the highest minimum payment first. This nameless method prioritizes the amount of money needed for your emergency fund so you don't have to include such a large payment in your emergency savings. No matter what method you decide to use, try to stick to it for a few months to see how it works. If you tried one for, I'll say three months, and it isn't working for you, feel free to shift to another. However, if you find yourself shifting methods often, it might be time to have an honest chat with yourself about what is actually going on and why it has been hard to stick to a method.

Financial education like this isn't the end-all be-all, but it is helpful in getting you started on the right track. The number of people I hear say "I should have known better" is jarring. My questions to you are "Why do you think that?" and "How could you have known?" For first-generation wealth builders, we may be the first people in our families to navigate life outside of survival or scarcity. You can't hold yourself accountable for things you didn't know you needed or didn't have a blueprint for.

So, What Now?

Thinking that something is wrong with you because your life doesn't look a certain way is for the birds. How boring would life be if we all did the same thing? While validation has its place in our lives, putting on for people is futile, and if we're being honest, keeping up with the Joneses says less about your neighbors, friends, and peers and more about how you want to be perceived. Again, even the Joneses have Joneses. That's the thing about money; there's always someone who has more. Do you think Elon Musk, Jeff Bezos, and the Arnault family reached a certain net worth and said, "Yeah, I am good here"? Nope. Their relationship with money dictates that they do more. Unfortunately, this is the kind of unsatisfying relationship with money that capitalism breeds. Learning to be content with life is extremely difficult, but it's necessary if you want to move beyond the next "get." Attempting to top people is a huge waste of your time, and sometimes it can be a surprising blow to your ego.

It can be easy to brush off your unhealthy financial habits if you don't see the damage being done, so let's take a step back for a minute and dig deeper. Are you getting deeper into debt? Are you mismanaging your money? What is causing you to spend so much? Is your lifestyle or cost of living the root of your issue? If you have an inkling that it might be emotional, you would be right. What are you trying to feel, or not feel, when you make a purchase? What emotion is your purpose fulfilling or helping you cope with? It doesn't always have to be tremendously deep, but more often than not, there is something there that needs to be addressed.

As we've learned, it's best to be brutally honest with yourself about how you feel about yourself, your life, and how others see you. Don't get me wrong, enjoying your money is extremely important, but it's not as important as being financially stable. If you can't afford a new car, a vacation, or new clothes, yet you are actively trading your future for it, it's time to make a change.

I want you to step off the hustle treadmill that encourages you to try to keep pace with everyone else. This kind of anxious thinking can quickly lead you to a place where you feel awful about yourself and how you live, perhaps driving you to drown in all the "wrong" choices you've seemingly made in the past. Stopping that thought pattern and living in gratitude is imperative to ending the vicious cycle of comparison. The hedonic treadmill, formerly known as hedonic adaptation, "is an adaptation-level phenomenon, which . . . describes how humans become insensitive to new stimuli, and quickly readjust to an emotional baseline . . . the stimulus needed to create an emotion—like happiness or excitement—[then] needs to be more intense than the last stimulus in order for someone to feel its effects."[43] This is important to think about when we talk about comparison because it can help explain the need for us to keep amping up our purchases and lifestyles or moving and adjusting the goal post of our success. Keeping up will always require you to chase something or someone in an effort to be "enough." But you are already more than enough, and you deserve to live a financially healthy life now. You always have.

While this chapter focused on debt, this is only the beginning. I encourage you to keep exploring your money beliefs as you continue working through this book and after. Make a list of what worries you and slowly start learning how to tackle each one. This slow but steady progress will help resolve some of the anxiety that comes with not knowing what to do with your money, though no amount of financial education will allow you to escape yourself. So above all else, continue to be honest with what you want and need to process, heal, and move forward.

Chapter 7

Money Hoarder

Serena had made the painstaking decision to leave New York City and move back home to England. While her heart knew it was the right decision, her brain struggled to keep up with the realities of what it took to move. It was not only a logistical nightmare, but also emotional. In one session with me, she discussed how telling people she was moving out of New York was like going through a breakup over and over again. For some this may feel extreme, but if you have ever moved from a place people are obsessed with, the sentiment holds true. It was also a move across an ocean, but she managed to make it happen. After having a proverbial goodbye tour, it was time to leave.

I saw Serena through her move, helped her transition into her new life, and assisted her in transferring her care to a new therapist. As we were going through the process of termination (therapist lingo for ending care), she said it felt like we were breaking up as well. She told me she most definitely wasn't settled, she was not ready to stop seeing me, and she wanted nothing to do with finding a new therapist. I understood. I enjoyed our work together and would have gladly kept working together. Unfortunately, rules are rules, and it was the law because she now lived in a different country.

Inside Scoop

Therapists are sad to end relationships with clients too—at least I am. Our clients feel connected to us, and we feel the connection too. Even when the timing is perfect and your client is ready to end their sessions, it can be hard and sad to say goodbye. I still send good vibes to clients I stopped working with years ago. I hope you are well!

As we were closing out our work together, Serena was simultaneously navigating major life decisions, one of which was buying a car. This may sound like a good time for the purchase, but for Serena, it was utterly anxiety provoking and paralyzing. Not only did she self-identify as "a shit decision maker," but she was also a money hoarder.

What the hell is a money hoarder? It is exactly what it sounds like. Someone who hoards their money, pinching pennies and squirreling away cash without any major plan but to use it on a rainy day. Usually this money is held in a checking or savings account, which is fine, though I pray it is at least a high yield savings account (HYSA). A money hoarder typically has thousands of dollars just sitting around, and oftentimes, it is far more money than they actually need.

This might not sound like a bad thing. I can hear you now. "Come on, Aja. If someone had loads of money, it sounds like they are in a great position. Where's the problem?" You are right! On one hand, having money saved *can* be great! It can provide many things, most notably comfort and safety. However, what happens when the fear and concern of overspending money paralyzes you? What happens if you never invest it, so it doesn't have a chance to really change your life? This is often the case with a money hoarder, and Serena was no different. She had tens of thousands of dollars sitting in her savings account, just chilling, collecting the crap interest rate of a traditional savings account.

Serena had enough money to purchase a car outright, yet she struggled to splurge on herself, even for smaller purchases. Buying a whole-ass car was outside of her realm of comfort. We had discussed the details of what type of car she wanted, what she felt like she could afford in comparison to her actual budget, and what it would look like to make the decision and buy it. She was concerned that she would make the wrong decision. Eventually, she found a car that checked all her boxes, and yet she still hesitated. "I don't feel like I have enough," she shared with me. Now, this is a huge purchase, and it can understandably take people time to get comfortable parting with that much money. But Serena had done all the research, knew it was well within her budget, and still continued to hesitate. Her money hoarding tendencies were getting in the way of her being great.

Something Deeper

You see, Serena had grown up in a household with financial stability, but she went through life with an overwhelming sense that something might happen to take it all away. Due to her family's history of substance use, Serena felt insecure about her family's ability to maintain financial security. She didn't trust that some major event wouldn't take the financial legs from under her family, subsequently leading to financial ruin. Nothing had happened to plant this fear, but anxiety is anxiety, and it's not always rational or logical. Whether realistic or not, Serena grew up wondering when the other shoe was going to drop, ever fearful of a major accident, unexpected medical bill, or surprise legal situation. With concern festering unchecked, she stashed cash like it was her job. For her, she was ensuring her safety for a rainy day, but what she didn't realize was that her anxiety and concern for financial safety were affecting her ability to truly thrive.

In our work together, we realized Serena was using large cash reserves to ensure safety and security in *all* aspects of her life. Her anxiety governed her decisions, and she always worried the people around her would not be able to show up for her if the need arose. She committed herself to saving and making sure she could keep herself safe. Some frivolously spend to cope with feelings of discomfort, but Serena saved her money to cope with hers. Spending it felt like it was in direct conflict with her safety. Although this was not true, she was often triggered by potential purchases, large and small. When we enter the stress cycle, our brain tells us to prioritize our safety (i.e., fight or flight). Our brains are so efficient at self-preservation that they don't stop to identify how big or small the threat is until a little later. This all happens at break-neck speed.

Serena's concern for her family, desire to maintain "enough" savings, and generalized anxiety created indecision and the perfect storm for her to be financially triggered when it came to buying a car. To get to this point of awareness, our work had to be done in layers. This took time, people, as it should with anyone. This is not something you can rush, though some of my past clients have made quality efforts to do just that. Here's what we did.

Our work together started with understanding the roots of Serena's anxiety, why it was there, and what purpose it was serving her. I know it's sometimes hard to believe that our anxiety or obsessive thinking serve any kind of purpose, but they usually do. Think of it as a misguided coping strategy. Healthy or not, it is there to help you cope with or relieve discomfort. Without diving into too much detail (because . . . nuance and confidentiality), Serena's anxiety was there to help her control things. Growing up in a household where things often felt chaotic and unspoken, Serena's ruminating and overthinking were all an attempt to prepare herself for what *might* happen. This happens frequently when the dynamics of a household are unstable. People experiencing anxiety can feel out of control, and to gain back some control of the situation or circumstance, they prepare for the unexpected, all with the hope that when something happens, they'll have nothing to worry about.

Upon digging into her relationship with money, I realized that uncertainty made Serena feel less safe. Her concern that no one in the house would truly be able to take care of her, whether true or not, fueled her anxiety even more. Although she was provided for physically, the emotional ways she specifically needed to be cared for weren't present. There had been little whiffs telling me that we needed to have a bigger, deeper conversation about money, but in therapy, sometimes you have to wait for the client to get there on their own. My approach is always person centered to understand their experiences, build connections, and see their pattern of behavior, all while letting my client slowly reveal when and where they are ready to go. Don't get me wrong, I will push my clients sometimes, but I know descending too quickly into the pain can be harmful, just like diving too fast into deep water. And that is exactly what you are doing when you start therapy, diving into the ocean of your experiences, psyche, and life. People aren't always ready to uncover how it all connects. It all takes time.

As we have discussed, understanding how the many layers of your life intertwine to impact your financial behaviors and decisions is paramount in shifting your relationship with money. You have to understand where you come from and what your beliefs are to then be able to rework and rewire your train of thought and cope in healthier ways. This is what doing the work looks like, friends: coming face-to-face with your feelings about things you didn't think mattered, you buried, or you were afraid to admit to yourself.

Squirreling Away Too Much

Through Serena's experience, hopefully you're beginning to understand that our beliefs about money are often a lot deeper than the numbers. Without realizing it, she and many other clients' desire to control their money by, seemingly, limiting any missteps manifests as fear and anxiety. Worrying that they won't have enough or will not have access to cash reserves should anything go wrong drives their money-hoarding behaviors. They are trying to limit risk, keep themselves safe, and ensure security in the future. Anxiety is all about control, whether or not it is realistic.

There is a place for fear and anxiety with your money, but like anything, too much of a good thing can be bad for you. Many of us are taught to save our money or stash it for a rainy day or worthy financial goals; however, we aren't always taught to balance saving with enjoying our money. Yes, I am telling you that in addition to saving money, you need to spend it, too. Enjoying your money is a healthy financial habit that needs to be cultivated, just as saving does.

Nothing rang truer than speaking to a friend's father who was struggling to set a date to retire. He very nonchalantly admitted to me that he had been saving all his life to retire and was a bit confused. Now he was just supposed to spend it? Um, yup! That is exactly what he should do. He should enjoy the fruits of his decades-long labor of investing, stashing, and compounding interest and live a comfortable life. So yes, again, for the people in the back, I want you to spend your money. Enjoy it, hang out with your loved ones, go on trips, and do all the things you said no to in the past.

Ramit Sethi's book and interactive journal of the same name, *I Will Teach You to Be Rich*, are dedicated to helping you understand your rich life. Making your best life a reality is going to cost money, so learning how to spend it to create the life you want is imperative. That is what I want for you: to understand yourself and your life and how your life experiences impact your money so you can shift the habits that need shifting and live your most authentic, rich life, whatever that means to you.

All the Feels: What's Happening Emotionally?

I want to take this opportunity to differentiate two key parts of this topic: financial stress and financial anxiety. **Financial stress** is born from feeling unstable in your finances. It could stem from specific situations, such as your family only giving you access to funds to pay your bills if you comply with their demands or leaving the financial support of your family and struggling to make ends meet to live out your dreams. These are but two examples; the possibilities are endless. Remember, it doesn't have to feel stressful to everyone for it to be stressful to you. I say this because we are often quick to belittle our experiences, assuming our scenario isn't as hard as someone else's or shouldn't be hard at all. Things can be hard with or without immense privilege.

Perhaps not surprisingly, financial stress is one of the top causes of stress in the United States.[44] While we all have a built-in system to help us navigate threats and stress, as we learned in chapter 5, the body was not meant to be exposed to prolonged periods of it, no matter where the stress is coming from. The hormones our body utilizes to manage the fight, flight, or freeze response were not made to be present indefinitely. The impacts of chronic stress, financial or otherwise, are immense, lingering, and expensive. We need to worry about not only the physical impact of stress but also the interruption it causes in your everyday life, at work, and in your relationships.

My friend Yemi Rose, founder of OfColor, a financial wellness platform designed to empower employees of color to build wealth, is working to combat this exact problem. When Yemi and I chatted about employee financial stress, he said, "Money is undefeated as the primary source of stress in America. This stress negatively impacts other aspects of well-being, such as physical health, mental health, and our relationships with friends and family . . . with financial shocks to the American economy seeming to come more frequently, feelings of financial insecurity have resulted in a very stressed workforce. Companies see the impact of these elevated stress levels in a number of areas, like employee burnout, reduced productivity, and higher retention and health care costs. But the real damage is to the worker."

When you are stressed, it is harder to show up for yourself and the people you care about. You may feel more irritable, have less patience, have trouble sleeping, or struggle to maintain healthy relationships that protect you from stress in the first place.

Alternatively, **financial anxiety** can come from a multitude of places: generalized anxiety, financial trauma, poverty, fear, and an infinite number of different life circumstances. Let's say, for instance, someone was hoarding their money, citing not knowing what to do with it as their rationale. While financial education and guidance are necessary, they don't address the emotional aspects of why you feel compelled to put off action. Fear is the root that needs to be addressed in this example—the fear that you might mess up, lose, or do something wrong. Truthfully, fear is an important emotion. It protects us and allows us to assess the safety and validity of our choices. It can motivate us, causing us to seek out new perspectives and force us into action. But fear can also keep us stuck, and it can be detrimental to our ability to grow wealth.

I say all this knowing that my ability to list all the potential examples where fear is either good or bad for your money is literally impossible; there will always be exceptions. But for the sake of this conversation, I want you to reflect on a time when fear stopped you from acting, pushing yourself toward a healthier you, or doing right by your future self and your money. Write your findings in a journal and refer to them and those unpleasant feelings whenever you feel this same resistance moving forward.

Anxiety is a tricky thing. Diagnosable generalized anxiety disorder has very specific symptoms, time frames, and behaviors that can only be diagnosed by licensed and trained providers. However, anxiety is part of the normal range of human emotion we all feel. It is further complicated when we get specific about what is going on. Financial anxiety is not specifically recognized by the *Diagnostic and Statistical Manual of Mental Disorders* (DSM), which does not recognize many financial-related behaviors outside of gambling disorder. This is why it may be hard for Americans to use health insurance to pay for financial therapy outside of being diagnosed with a gambling disorder. Not to mention, mental health providers are not required to receive training in money psychology, financial therapy, or behavioral economics.

Both financial stress and anxiety can result in financial trauma. I spoke to my friend Rahkim Sabree, *Forbes* columnist and financial therapist, to chat about his thoughts on financial trauma. He noted:

> *People are focusing on its impact due to heightened awareness around the complexities of mental health, and the championing of those who connect the dots between financial education and the expected resulting behavior being influenced by variables like culture, values, psychology, and generational trauma.*
>
> *As the personal finance landscape and those who represent it change—introducing diversity of thought and experiences to the equation—it's becoming much more difficult to ignore the fact that everyone's interactions with money differ, and more importantly, it shines a light on the systemic and structural inequality that gives some a huge advantage and others a hole to dig out of.*

The thing about trauma is we so frequently want to ignore the magnitude and potential longevity of its impact. It can feel safer and more comfortable to bury it deep inside of us, pretending it will stay there untouched, never to cause us harm again. Unfortunately, for humans, that is rarely the case. A part of us is forever changed because of what we experience, and this goes for any type of trauma, not only financial. As tempting as it may be to neglect your trauma, you can't. It always makes itself known, usually at inopportune moments.

My clients have often asked me why we have to go back to those hard feelings to examine the past. For me, it's less about the details of the event and more about giving voice to how you felt and internalized what you went through. What you thought and felt during that time quickly becomes a narrative you hold yourself to, often well beyond the event and without your even noticing. In freeing the hurt part of yourself you locked away, you allow your feelings to be known, validated, and honored. And ironically, feeling this pain and letting it flow through and out of you is what can allow you to finally be free from it. This is why we go back, not so you can change the past (because you can't) or wallow in self-pity, but so you can change the impact that pain will have on your future self. That is who we do this work for, who we are protecting and looking out for: the future you. In this way, you can become aware of those feelings and triggers, honor them properly, and manage them better when they bubble up to the surface because they eventually will.

Any combination of these deep-seated feelings and traumatic experiences can lead someone to hoard their money. But money freedom is possible. With the many money activities and strategies I discuss in this book, you can enjoy your money freely. I know this is often easier said than done. Ever since the TikTok gurus found out people had the power to shift how they think and feel by replacing negative thoughts with positive ones, social media has been ablaze. Now, I love a manifestation moment as much as the next person, but I also know there can be a lot of real complexities that come with our financial beliefs and stories. Healing from scarcity, hardships, wage gaps, and systemic oppression takes a lot of work, and while believing in yourself and the universe to bring good things is extremely important, it's sometimes not enough to just think positively. When you are in a place of survival, scarcity makes it harder to believe manifesting abundance is possible for you. You cannot heal from the same damage you are currently trying to survive. Yes, knowing what you want, striving toward it, and reframing your thoughts are all powerful, but you also need to understand some basic personal finance behaviors, how to implement them in your life, and how your past has impacted what you do with your money today. Once you've gotten all those bases covered, then by all means let your manifestation practice fly.

Let's Get Financial: A Lesson in Money

So frequently our parents or elders tell us to "save, save, save," but most times they don't tell us why we should be saving, what we should saving for, or what constitutes a rainy day. This is where financial education comes in. When you are properly informed, you can decide what your goals are instead of allowing other people to govern what you do with your money. When you do not have appropriate financial education, it can be easy to fall into the trap of blindly doing what others around you are doing. Now, if they are rocking their finances, by all means replicate that; however, if they also do not know how money works, you must be the one to correct your path. I am not here to knock those around you, but sometimes doing what your parents told you to do or doing what they did can be detrimental, and you wouldn't know that unless you had the financial education to make different money moves.

Learning what you don't know is the key. No one has time to miss opportunities to grow wealth.

And no one has time to have their emotions get in the way of their happiness, either. To do so, let's get real about what effective saving looks like and learn a little about accounts. Like spending plans, I don't think there is any right or wrong way to manage your savings, but I do believe there are ways that may be better for you and your money. You choose the way; I am here to give you some options. Whether it be a digital bank for those of you who are not close to a brick-and-mortar bank or the opportunity to meet with a financial professional, deciding where you put your money is all about preference. Here are some options for the types accounts you may have access to, depending on where you choose to store your money:

- **Checking accounts.** These accounts are tied to your debit card and are typically where you pay your bills from, store your spending money, and so on.
- **Traditional savings accounts.** These accounts are sometimes tied to a checking account and oftentimes offer a very low interest rate for the money you store in them, generally 0.05 to 1 percent. This means the bank will give you a

teeny, tiny percentage to have your cash stored in their savings account. These numbers are abysmal compared to the potential of a high yield savings account.

- **High yield savings accounts (HYSAs).** These savings accounts work the same as a traditional savings account; however, their interest rates are much higher (generally 3 to 5 percent), which allows you to earn more money for simply having your money in the account. Remember the power of compounding interest? This is a time when it is your friend. Having your money work for you is a glorious wealth hack, even if it is only adding up a little bit at a time. While HYSAs are overwhelmingly available via online or digital banks, there are some brick-and-mortar locations that offer them. If you'd prefer a physical location you can go to, check around at your local credit unions to see which ones offer HYSAs.
- **Certificate of deposit (CD).** These are banking products attached to a bank or bank account that allow you to deposit a sum of money that you agree to not touch for a specific time frame. In exchange, you are given a large interest rate (2 to 5 percent) to help grow your money even faster. Essentially, you are letting the bank

borrow your money in exchange for a high interest rate. The only catch is you cannot touch or move the cash for an allotted period.

Now that you have some foundational information about the kinds of accounts you can keep your money in, let's discuss how to use them. As a rule of thumb, you should aim to keep a certain amount of money easily accessible for those "just in case" moments, the proverbial rainy days, or unexpected emergencies. This is what your savings is for; I don't want you saving "just because" anymore because you will be saving forever without purpose. Over here, we are intentional about our financial wellness, health, and priorities.

Your emergency, "fuck it" fund, or "just in case" money is for when you need to pay an unexpected expense (a medical bill, keeping yourself afloat after job loss, car repairs, unexpectedly leaving a relationship, etc.). This fund is best stored in a high yield savings account. To be clear, these funds are not for the surprise trip with your besties or to get the latest iPhone. Hands off, emergencies only! There is a lot of debate about how much money should be in this fund. The amount I hear most frequently is three to six months' worth of expenses. You can find your number by going back to the action steps of chapters 4 and 5. When you tally up where you are financially and what your monthly spend is, you will be able to come up with the number needed in your savings account. Multiply whatever it costs to maintain your lifestyle each month by the number of months you are looking to have saved in your emergency fund. For example, if it costs you $5,000 a month to live and you want a three-month emergency fund, you will work to store $15,000 ($5,000 × 3) in your HYSA. If you would feel comfortable with more money, like six months' worth of savings, you would aim to store $30,000 ($5,000 × 6).

I have frequently read that if you work for yourself, have a family, or work in a high-turnover field, you should save about six to twelve months' worth of savings in your emergency fund to remain comfortable if anything comes up. I will let you decide what your level of risk is and what feels most comfortable to you, but I would suggest, at the very least, you have three months of expenses saved. If, for any reason, you or your family experience a loss in income, you know you can survive for at least three months. To come up with a number that makes the most sense for you, consider the following: How much cushion would you like to have if anything happened to your income? How many months would it take you to find a new job or start making an income with a new business venture?

This is a lot of money to save. For many of us, saving this amount of cash may not only take a long time but also feel impossible with our current circumstances. I don't like to use words like *impossible*, but the time, discipline, and effort can feel like you are climbing Mount Everest without the necessary gear. There is hope. Recent research has suggested that even saving around $2,500 would be helpful in protecting people from falling behind in their bills or taking on more debt.[45] Once you have an emergency fund of any size saved, you may be interested in saving for other things. Sinking funds, which are amounts of money saved for specific causes, like Beyoncé tickets, a vacation, that annual sale, a new car, or other purchases throughout the year, can help keep you from dipping into your emergency fund. This money can live within the same account as your emergency fund or in a different savings account, but it will be important for you to know what money is earmarked for what. Some banks offer buckets, or savings goals, that digitally track what your money is being saved for. Giving each bucket a name will help remind you of what you are saving for and why it is so important to you.

Example Savings Split:
Emergency fund (three months of expenses):
$15,000
Vacation: $5,000
Pet fund: $2,000
Car repair: $4,000

All that money might live in the same HYSA, but with buckets or savings goals, you know certain amounts are for specific things.

Next Steps

There are many ways to save: sending a certain dollar amount or percentage to your savings account through automatic deposit, manually moving money each pay period, or immediately moving the difference between what you budgeted for and what you spent. If you are in a position where you don't have a lot of money coming in, saving any amount can be helpful. So even if you only move $5 one month and $20 the next, something is always going to be better than nothing. Once you have reached your emergency savings goal and have set aside enough money for your sinking funds, *stop* saving. Yes, I said it. We are no longer saving for the sake of saving. I would much rather you start directing that money toward growing your wealth through investing. The urge to continuously save may be there, but that is how money hoarding can get out of hand. Figure out how much you need and to feel comfortable for an emergency fund, whether that be $2,500, three months of expenses, or a number you just like to see. Then decide what extras or yearly expenses you want to save for. After you reach those numbers, it is time to focus on growing your money instead. Let the compound interest of your HYSA do the work and move on to something else.

Even for those of us who are money hoarders, having the appropriate accounts to store our money will be helpful in our quest for financial wellness, as will being aware of your money behaviors.

Serena and I eventually ended our work together, and a few months later, she contacted me to let me know she did, in fact, find a new therapist. She thanked me for the work we had done together and noted that her new therapist was challenging her just as much as I did. She also shared how proud she was of herself and how much she loved driving her brand-new car.

Reflection Questions

A few reflection questions to guide you:

- What are your initial thoughts around saving?
- Do you have a hard time spending your money? Why do you think that is?
- Was there a purchase you denied yourself because you thought it was too expensive or not important enough?
- Can you remember a time in your life when you were concerned about money? What strategies have you put in place to keep you financially safe?

If you relate to Serena's money hoarding behaviors, please know that you can experience the same level of money freedom and truly enjoy your hard-earned cash with zero guilt or regret. Take your time uncovering your past hurts, and give yourself grace with what you find. You are capable of releasing yourself from the financial confines you've found yourself in.

Chapter 8

You Are What You Do

I was recently at a friend's house for a gathering, and upon introducing ourselves, another woman asked me what I liked to do before I became a mom. What a good question! Of course, I currently have a life outside of motherhood, but as most parents can tell you, the way you spend your time after taking on this new identity as a parent is often dramatically different. It certainly has been for me. I appreciated that this person tried to get to know me both outside of and alongside my identity as a mom and didn't immediately start the conversation by asking what I do for work, which is often how most people strike up conversations with new people. This is particularly important for parents. Our identities shift so much when tiny humans come into our lives. It is a beautiful yet difficult restructuring of priorities. You can lose yourself in parenting itself, and outside of your household, you are frequently reduced to the parent of [insert child's name here]. You and your name are gone. And it is not only children who commit this seemingly benign crime of passion; many adults are guilty of the same thing, myself included. I often find myself referring to my husband as "Daddy" (and not in a sexy way) or myself in the third person as "Mommy." My identity as Aja now has many layers and is frequently being reprioritized.

This is but one example of how what you spend your time doing informs aspects of your identity. Outside of parenthood, your profession and how you make money can make up far too much of your identity. One of the first questions people ask when trying to get to know one another is "So what do you do?" I have most definitely fallen victim to this line of questioning. As more attention has been brought to how detrimental hustle culture is, spending time on yourself outside of work has become the antidote. "In an unhealthy workplace culture, employees often feel compelled to go above and beyond in ways that harm their well-being, such as by taking on additional projects that cause them to miss out on important family or social events," said Anthony C. Klotz and Mark C. Bolino in their piece for the *Harvard Business Review*.[46] This begs the question: *Are* you what you do? And, by extension, are you what you earn?

More often than not, people measure their success by what they "do." One's job or career can sometimes make up their entire identity, how they provide, who they believe themselves to be, or how they show up for others. A big part of this is related to the financial markers associated with success. It becomes the glue holding their house of cards together. I assure you, if someone else has identified you as old enough to be an adult, you have most likely felt like your life was a house of cards built on a hope and a prayer that you are actually responsible and capable enough to handle the responsibilities you have somehow been entrusted with. I recently heard someone say, "Adulting is feeling the difference in age in your body but mentally feeling like you are still twenty-two." Except at thirty-six, you remember what your body did at twenty-two and what it feels like to do those same things nearly fifteen years later. You don't always forget your responsibilities with your chosen vice. If you are lucky, you just have more money to try to make it all happen. Most of us are looking around wondering where the "real" adults are, only to realize *we* are the real adults. The only person coming to save you is you!

After the height of the COVID-19 pandemic, people seemed to wake up and move away from "living to work" toward "working to live." That harsh disruption to our lives in 2020 made a lot of us take a harder look at the way we were living, and as a result, people are no longer hell-bent on assessing the social standing of someone solely based on their job. In a BBC piece titled "Why You Shouldn't Ask People

What They Do," Al Gini, author of *My Job, My Self*, shared that "retaining a distinct identity causes less grief during a job loss, creates more authentic connections outside of the office and helps people feel more respected even when away from a powerful job. But as companies require a full-time connection to work, many workers find themselves unable to separate their identity from what they do professionally. This may ultimately negatively affect their well-being."[47] I have found what Gini said to be true.

So, I stopped asking "What do you *do*?" as one of my leading questions, which allows the other person an opportunity to decide how they want others to see them. I am sure not everyone is thinking about it this hard (blame it on my day job!), but I've found that shifting the phrasing to "What do you do for work?" allows their professional work to be shared as an *aspect* of their life rather than their sole identity. I am here to tell you that the notion of "you are what you do" is a thing of the past, friends. What someone does for work and how they make their money no longer quantifies who they are as a whole person. Unfortunately, many people have yet to receive this memo.

Picture This

I had been working with Ruth, a Haitian American woman, for six months before she decided to quit her grueling job, which often required her to work sixty hours on a good week and upward of eighty or more when shit was really crazy. Before making the jump, she frequently shared that the path set out for her was one she didn't really want. She wasn't sure if she was ready to commit herself to this work for the long term. Not only were the hours a problem, but so were her feelings about work. This isn't to say that we all need to be filled with passion for our jobs; there are plenty of people who are perfectly committed to work without it being something they intrinsically care about. However, for Ruth, it was important to feel a spark for what she was doing. She wanted to feel connected to work. What she didn't know yet was that she actually wanted to feel connected to herself.

Ruth was raised in a household that emphasized the importance of education and the prestige of a stable career, so she committed herself to doing it all the "right way." She checked the boxes, earning good grades, being involved at school, showing up for her family, and at church. If you know Caribbean families (and many other immigrant families raising first-generation Americans), you know telling them you are shifting out of a "good" job because you are unhappy isn't always met with positivity and understanding. Daring to step outside the path your elders worked so hard to create for you brings a lot of feelings to the surface, not only within yourself but from those around you. Not everyone will understand or support your desire to make drastic changes to find yourself. Lack of social support only makes the journey more difficult. Despite these factors, Ruth knew she had to find whatever was missing. She took the time to be open and allow her needs to reveal themselves. The disconnect she felt in her life made it clear that something needed to change. She did not want to feel lost in her life a second longer, so I joined her on the quest to not only think outside of the box professionally but find what she really wanted.

If you know me personally, you know I will blow up my entire life to maintain my mental and emotional stability. When I was twenty-six years old, I realized I was depressed after having a "menty b" (Gen Z speak for mental breakdown) in front of my coworkers. I didn't realize it, but I had completely lost myself to my job and responsibility as a clinician. I was duller, some might say numb. It embarrassingly took months and someone else calling me out for me to realize I was depressed. So, I blew up my life. I quit my job, left a budding relationship, and moved to Barcelona for two months. I came back only for the holidays before jumping the pond to go back to Europe for three months. I had to figure my shit out!

I share this because although I was able to do this, not everyone has the luxury and privilege to do so; and honestly, I barely did either. (I spent all my savings and had a large credit card bill afterward.) We do not all have the insight or bravery to realize something needs to drastically change in how we are living, nor do we all have the financial means to upend our life in such a dramatic fashion. Like me and countless others, my client Ruth needed to make a change and shake things up. Before she quit, she talked to me and countless friends to make sure she could financially weather a couple of months of unemployment. Welp! A couple of months of unemployment turned into one of the hardest years of self-growth she had ever experienced.

A little aside: The importance of an emergency fund cannot be overstated. If you are like Ruth and want to bust out of your job, having a savings cushion to do so will save your mental health. This also goes for job loss! Being financially prepared only gives you *more* options.

We dismantled how much of her identity was attached to her title and who she felt she had become at her last job. She was playing by the rules, but the game, she realized, was not about her. We spent that year nurturing her self-esteem, desires, wants, and needs and cultivating an image of what she wanted her future to look like. During that time, she realized how much of her life was built in service to other people. How frequently she abandoned her needs to show up for someone else. While acts of service were most certainly her love language, over time they had begun to crowd out her own wants. She worked on connecting the value she inherently brought to the world outside of her job, bringing the qualities of her personality forward. She dove into taking care of her body, finding hobbies that brought her joy, and relearning how to enjoy her alone time without the pressure to fill it. She learned that she not only wanted more balance in her life but also required it. Gone were the days of Ruth working tirelessly day in and day out, and present was the importance of having time to spend with friends and family, at the gym, or in her own company at home.

She was successful in her journey to uncouple her worth and identity from her profession. When Ruth finally found work, it was in a different industry and came with a 50 percent pay cut. Although she wanted the job, Ruth was not prepared for the financial and mental implications of such a drastic shift. On top of the work we were doing to strengthen her identity outside of work, we also had to work on how she could feel like herself without some of the comforts she had become accustomed to.

She had to learn to live on less, be more mindful of where her money went, and come to terms with how she was seen by strangers. These were fairly easy switches for her, but what was harder was what came next: the social components. Would her friends still invite her if she couldn't afford to go on vacation? Was she just as professional if she didn't have new clothes for her job or beautifully manicured nails? Would her family be disappointed if she didn't have her fancy title? The shift in job and financial standing had Ruth questioning the work we had done together. Deep down, she knew the answer to all her questions. She liked her new job and was ready for a challenge, but she was financially stressed. Even though she wanted it, it still felt uncomfortable and came with a level of reckoning she had not yet made peace with.

Ruth realized a main component to how she saw herself was wrapped up in how much her net worth was attached to her self-worth. It was more than she was prepared to admit at first, but with time, she was ready. She continued to deepen her understanding of her most authentic self and dissect her relationship with money. Getting to know herself on a deeper level paved the way for her to slowly fall in love with herself again. I get emotional thinking about it. I know how hard she was working and what she was giving and searching for, led only by the hope that one day she would be better off for doing all of this. Supporting someone on this journey is an honor. To walk with Ruth and all my clients as they navigate growing into their truest self and shifting their life to make room for that person is some of the most rewarding work of my career. Some would call it self-actualization, but really, it's an evolution into a more understanding and insightful version of oneself. That's what therapy is for.

All the Feels: Boundaries and Your Family

In chapter 3, we discussed the importance of being a part of a community and how these connections are built into the cultural fabric of BIPOC culture. Whether it be with your immediate family or surrounding community, acceptance is a major part of belonging; however, staying in good standing with your community (no matter what culture you come from) may require you to not rock the boat or take any action that would appear too different from the limits of what's "normal." Staying within the parameters of what is acceptable often leads people to abandon themselves to seek or maintain approval from their peers, community, and most frequently, parents. The fear of rejection, conflict, or otherwise often leads to people-pleasing behaviors. There is a place for respecting your elders, wanting to make your parents proud, giving back to the family, and maintaining the safety of the group. Where I encourage you to begin thinking introspectively about what does and doesn't work for you is when the community's definition of acceptable differs vastly from how you would like to live your life. Staying in a job you hate for the sake of your family is not it. Neither is being miserable to appease others. For some, this may come with serious financial repercussions, which is why financial wellness is so important. If you have to sacrifice your mental or physical well-being or authenticity for acceptance, that community is no longer safe for you. Instead, I argue that your motivating factor for staying is fear, and that is okay because doing something different from the norm is often scary. The potential heartbreak of losing those closest to you because of the conflict between who you are and who they want you to be is devastating; however, staying may be just as dangerous.

Disclaimer: There is privilege in being able to create space between yourself and your community if it is stifling you.

Hiding who you are will never get you where you want to be. You may achieve the goal on the outside, but feeling miserable and hating yourself along the way isn't worth it. It tears people up inside to keep who they are a secret. That is no way to live. Now, taking the steps to remain authentic and remove yourself from unsupportive communities will take time. I am not telling you to blow up your life in service of your most authentic self. Rather, take the time to listen, learn as much as possible, figure out what you want life to look like, and then make slow, deliberate changes to get there. Shredding people-pleasing behaviors is complex when it is built into the culture of belonging, whether to a family, job, or otherwise. Change is scary and made even scarier when it feels like you are going against everything you have known.

For Ruth to live her authentic truth, she had to walk through the discomfort of her family not understanding why she had to make a change. The frequent branding of "putting your desires first" as selfish has caused many people to look down on self-care. The "one for all and all for one" mentality doesn't always leave space and time for introspection of the individual. Nothing is more beautiful to me than community-based cultures that look out for the interests of everyone—but not when it's to the detriment of the individuals in the community. The number of people I see who have a clearer definition of what their parents want for them rather than what they want for themselves is heartbreaking. If this sounds like you, I want you to know you can build a life that is both respectful of your needs and those of your community.

There is something to be said here about the potential implications of leaving a community, family, or relationship. There is a level of privilege in understanding that your needs have to be met in order to make a shift, and that, for most people, is what stops them. Many people are not in the financial position to leave, and let's be clear, I am not suggesting that for everyone. Financial abuse is a real thing. And on top of that, there are mental and emotional implications for making such a leap.

I have worked with a few people who have had to reckon with what a shift in, out, or beyond their job title has meant for their self-esteem. Whether it be through job loss or resigning, doing the work to figure out who you are outside of your job can get dark. Your self-esteem can suffer when you have been unemployed for longer than you originally planned for. There is a lot wrapped up in searching for a job that can leave people feeling like they aren't worthy, like competing with others to get positions, managing rejection, and constantly having to build yourself back up to continue applying. It is a very time-consuming process, and depending on how you do it, it can end up feeling like a job in and of itself. For some, it inadvertently causes an identity crisis. They are often forced to live their lives differently as they watch their savings dwindle. That shit is hard and possibly very triggering, as it seems like the sense of safety and security they spent time building is in danger. That is when people make rash, desperate decisions.

When you are financially triggered in this way, the discomfort you once successfully navigated in the past can come back as if you are going through it for the first time. This is yet another time when our psyche can interrupt what we want to do with our money. You may not always understand what is happening in your mind and body during these times, but that's where understanding yourself, your history, and how you react to new situations can serve you. This is why it's important to allow yourself to go through the stress cycle from chapters 3 and 5. It can stop you from making rash decisions with your money during a time of distress. We often think action is the best step when we are upset, but more often than not, we're being given an opportunity to pause, breathe, regulate our bodies (calm the fuck down), and reassess whether our plan is actually working or if we need to do something different. Abandoning your plan anytime you are triggered could have you spinning your financial wheels forever, and no one wants that when we are trying to get and grow this money.

We all have habits that help us regulate and cope when we are upset. For Serena, it was hoarding money. The fashion girlies may buy clothes. For my fellow Target babes, it may be spending in general. In the name of coping, people may engage in a number of different behaviors. I have learned that people usually do not realize they need to do this work before they are face-to-face with it. They don't see how much of their life is or was built around the demands of their job or how they are coping through the use of money.

Money's Impact

So, is what we do for work as much a part of our identity as how much money we make? Do people feel less than based on what their income is, or do they feel less than based on what they are able to buy or not? I can't say for sure because, honestly, sometimes it is a combination of both. Either way, it is an important conversation to have. What we do for work often dictates what our income might be, and that alone can be wrapped up in a slew of feelings. In many communities, people have given a six-figure salary the golden stamp of success. Reaching that income level supposedly cements your financial stability. In other words, if only I could reach this amount of money—$100,000, say—I would be all set. Although $100,000 is nearly double the average American income, it doesn't actually matter how much money you have or don't have. What matters is your relationship with money, how it impacts you, how it makes you feel, and how you see yourself in relation to it. How many times have we seen high-paid athletes, entertainers, and businesspeople file for bankruptcy or blow their wealth? This goes to show that it's not about the amount of money you make but what you do with it.

In Morgan Housel's book *The Psychology of Money*, he shared, "I thought they [luxury cars] sent such a strong signal to others that you made it. You're smart. You're rich. You have taste. You're important. Look at me. The irony is I rarely . . . look at them, the drivers." He goes on to lament about how frequently the driver thinks other people will make assumptions about them, who they are, and their success, when in reality, people are thinking to themselves, *Wow, if I had that car, people would think I'm cool.* Housel shares his thoughts on this paradox: "People tend to want wealth to signal to others that they should be liked and admired. But in reality, those other people often bypass admiring you, not because they don't think wealth is admirable, but because they use your wealth as a benchmark for their own desire to be liked or admired."[48]

Housel is right. People will go to great lengths to serve their self-esteem, whether it helps or not. Chasing more degrees or certifications to feel more comfortable calling themselves an expert. Bending over backward for their job, only to be passed over for a promotion. Going into a career they hate, thinking the approval of their parents, friends, or potential mate will cure how they feel about themselves. Going into debt chasing the status symbol they believe is going to show everyone that they have made it. The examples are endless, and these wealth signifiers rarely mean as much to other people as they do to the person who purchased them. And listen, I am all about you having all of this and more, if that is what truly makes you happy, but if you are doing so solely for the validation of other people, I have to break the unfortunate news to you: That will not work. You will find yourself constantly chasing the next big thing, never to be satisfied. The real freedom lies within.

Reflection Questions

- How much of your worth is connected to what you do for work? Would you feel confident in who you are if you had a different career path?
- Do you feel like your success is only connected to how much money you make or your title? Outside of finances, how else are you successful in life?
- How much of your self-worth is connected to how much you do for other people?
- What do you offer the world outside of your profession?

Let's Get Financial: Lesson in Money

Two things need to happen when you are trying to move past the negativity of thinking that all you have to offer is centered around your work or salary: First, you need to know who you truly are outside of work, and second, you need to create a financial plan that aligns with that vision of self. Let's begin by doing a bit of self-reflection.

Find a quiet place to sit down with your journal and reflect on the following questions: Who are you outside of your work? How do you show people who you are in your actions? Does what you portray on the outside match what's on the inside? What stops you from being your truest self?

Now that you've gotten a bit clearer on who you are, let's focus on creating a space where your money can support you, what you enjoy in life, and the goals you have for yourself. This is your self-made financial plan, a step-by-step path that will help you achieve your goals. Whenever you are creating a plan for your money and looking to understand what you want your financial health and wellness to look like, it is important to understand what *you* want, not what others want for you. So, first consider the following questions:

- What do you need to feel stable and secure?
- What do you want to accomplish financially?
- What would you enjoy being able to do more often?

You see what I did there: Your needs, wants, and enjoyment are the focus! That is what money should be to all of us, a tool that allows us to get our needs taken care of, our wants satisfied, and an opportunity for us to enjoy it. Too frequently we sacrifice one part of the equation for the other.

If you answer each of these questions honestly, you are well on your way to creating the foundation of a plan. Knowing you have an emergency fund saved, are working to pay off your debt, or are managing your money to achieve your goals can give you peace of mind when unexpected things happen. Life is going to life no matter what—a plan for your money allows you to feel more stable in your ability to handle such events. It will help regulate financial stress and anxiety when you find yourself financially triggered or at a loss for what to do. Your plan grounds you in action steps and execution. It can be as elaborate as you'd like. You can house it in a beautifully crafted Excel spreadsheet, in an app, or with good old pen and paper (my personal favorite). Whichever you choose is fine as long as it is documented somewhere where you will see it and use it.

Additionally, your budget is a part of this plan. It informs your day-to-day plan to funnel your money toward the goals that are in your overall macro financial plan for your money. Think of your budget as a tool to help execute on your overall larger plan, encompassing both the short and long term. This can also include your goals like saving, retirement, and everything you may want to accomplish financially in life. It sets you up to know and understand the order in which you want to accomplish things and check them off the list.

Here is an example of what someone's money plan might look like:

1. Save $3,000 for an emergency fund.
2. Create and commit to a realistic budget.
3. Start maxing out employee 401(k).
4. Use extra $325 (+$150 minimum payment) from sticking to the budget to pay off the $5,600 credit card.
5. Save three months of expenses for emergency fund.
6. Start saving for trip to Thailand with bestie.

I know we talked a little about this in chapters 6 and 7, but it bears repeating: Once you have a vague idea of what you want your financial life to look like, it is time to figure out how to do it. Look through your list of priorities—is there anything on there that you feel like you need more information about? Is there anything you don't feel knowledgeable or confident in your ability to make happen? What do you need to learn more about to be able to take the necessary steps?

I can't stress this enough: You cannot only rely on financial education to carry you to financial wellness! It is not enough and will not work. If you have read this far, you know that money is emotional. It is layered with life experience, and our emotions do not give two hot shits about math when our brains and bodies are telling us we *need* something. They will not always make sense, and they most definitely will not always be rational.

With that being said, financial education is necessary. You don't know what you don't know, and if financial knowledge and education make you slightly more confident in your ability to get your needs, wants, and enjoyment met, then that is a win. Admittedly, financial education has historically been notoriously very white. My friend Berna Anat has referred to past financial advice as "hella male, hella pale, and hella stale." She isn't wrong. Before the beautiful wave of diversity and intersectionality disrupted the personal finance landscape, we were stuck with a lot of people who looked the same and spoke to one experience. We know that just won't do. With social media connecting us every day, the diversity in experience and thought has been fantastic. However, I will caution you to be mindful of who you take financial advice from. Please fact-check all information and ensure that you are not being taken advantage of or misled into potentially catastrophic financial decisions.

I hope by now you understand that you are so much more than what you do. How you enjoy yourself, how you spend your time, and what makes you smile and tick are all small pieces of the whole that is you. Sometimes these "getting to know you" questions focused on work are for the sake of small talk, but other times they immediately limit the person standing in front of you. It's important that we begin to step away from this line of thinking and get a little more creative when we're looking to build long-term relationships or even uncover the truth of who we are.

I'll close with this quote from Al Gini: "The less we have in other interests, the more dependent we are on our job. So when we lose it, you totally fall apart."[49] We can feel trapped in the parts of our lives that feel forward facing; the things that are done in front of people can be the only information garnered, and that's not necessarily our truth. A community that supports you as your true self is a community you should aim to be a part of. Anything else is damaging to your self-esteem and long-term goals. So, make sure you are creating time, money, and energy to both pour into others and be poured into. It's good for all of us.

Chapter 9

Bring Us Home

It is unfortunate that the human condition dictates we experience both pain and pleasure. Nothing slaps you harder in the face with this reality than learning what adulthood *actually* entails. As children, there is a naivete in understanding what it takes to manage your life when you are responsible for it all. The freedoms of adulthood appear so enticing, so much so that many of us are ready to abandon our youth in hope of being taken more seriously and being treated as adults. This phenomenon is particularly present when we start talking about the often taboo subject of money. Whether you grew up with a lack of responsibilities or you felt the pains of having to go without, the beauty of inexperience often makes us feel like we have the solution. To children, getting older looks like you are always taken seriously, there are no rules, you govern whatever you want, and somehow it just all works out. Once we grow up, though, reality can be a tough pill to swallow: The landscape of adulting looks and feels a lot different than most of us anticipated. In addition to managing your own needs, you must also handle schedules, navigate relationships, chase your dreams, take care of your physical and mental health, and hope you like yourself and your life at the end of the day. That alone can be exhausting. Sprinkle on the potential financial stressors of debt, inflation, and a high cost of living, and many of us feel like the cards are stacked against us. Of course, not everyone has to deal with *concerns* about money, but everyone does have to deal with money.

As we've discussed throughout the book, our innate psychology dictates that we find a place of belonging to survive and thrive. There is a reason we often say "It takes a village" when referring to raising tiny humans. But honestly, we need a village at all stages of life. We all, no matter our age, want and need to belong in some capacity. To love and be loved is part of our human condition. We all need community (love/acceptance/nurturing), stability, and security. These are basic human needs. Unfortunately, given the loneliness epidemic that the COVID-19 pandemic exacerbated and the individual-focused nature of modern society, we need to course correct.[50] We have brushed aside the importance of community in our survival and have dug in our heels on not being vulnerable. It's not working. Money, as with many other things, is used to differentiate. This doesn't have to be the case if we do the work from last chapter and separate our net worth from our self-worth. If we look at people as inherently valuable, regardless of what they do for work or how much they money they make, it can shift the narrative from potentially divisive to unifying. To make this shift happen, though, we have to talk about it. We have to acknowledge all the hard topics, not only money. Only then can we humanize people and celebrate our differences rather than ostracize each other because of them.

History is fraught with examples of how damaging it is for us to segregate groups from the greater collective. We are still paying the price. The eternal optimist part of me wants to believe my utopian dreams of equality and harmony are possible. Can you imagine the economic power we'd have if only more people were given access and opportunity? I know there are a lot of people who believe the pie is only so big, but I am not one of them. I wholeheartedly believe there is enough room for all of us; after all, a rising tide lifts all boats. I want that tide to be an economic one.

I want people to see themselves in those they look up to. To see people who not only look like them but also look different from one another. I am not referring to only racial, gender, and religious diversity, but to a variety of differences, especially economic. Those differences, in conjunction with our similarities, is what representation is all about. Although I have had many privileges in my life, I don't think I will ever escape the expectation of hardship people assume I went through. As I said before, I have definitely lived through some shit, but the look of awe when I discuss my upbringing never ceases to amaze me. Walking around in my identity as a Black woman means some people will assume things about my life, family, and history that I have never experienced. Even if the expected hardship was part of my story, I am not certain anyone wants to hear all their accomplishments being chalked up to one aspect of their life, true or not. Those limiting beliefs in my capabilities fuel my ambition to this day.

For decades, women, especially Black women, have been told we need to shrink. Be small, easily digestible, and always likable. I am ready to burn that sentiment to the ground. If anyone ever requires you to abandon yourself in search of their comfort, I give you permission to literally and/or figuratively tell them to fuck off. As the wise Coco Gauff said when she won the 2023 US Open, "To those who thought they were putting water on my fire, you were really adding gas."[51] Looking at the clips of a younger Coco having a great time at the very stadium she would go on to win a Grand Slam at is what representation is all about. Venus and Serena Williams were a part of Coco's story—providing representation for her and so many of us, showing up and being present, reminding us that we could do it, too. You, too, can achieve it, whatever the "it" is for you.

Take the time to find out who you are and who you want to be, and when you do, love that version of yourself fiercely.

Protect yourself. I hope, after reading this book, you better understand not only yourself but your relationship to money. At the very least, I hope you've learned that your individual path to financial wellness is dictated not by how much financial education you have or how much money you make but by how much you understand the connections between your life experiences and how you behave with money. In a world where money has dictated so much, I want this book to be a catalyst for you, a beacon of representation that not only says "You can do it, too" but also shows you what you need to do and how to heal from your financial stressors and challenges. As insidious as greed can be, money itself is a needed resource.

As we end our time together for now, know that we aren't breaking up for good! I am still here and would love to keep in touch. Feel free to reach out via my newsletter or on social media (@ajaetherapy). Now, let's wrap this up by going through the steps to ensure you know how to become financially well.

Your Guide to Financial Wellness Starts Here

Whether knowingly or not, you have already walked this path as you've journeyed through the book, but sometimes, as with therapy, things bear repeating to see the forest from the trees.

Step 1: Get honest with yourself, your life, and your limiting beliefs.

Everything you do with money is built from the financial experiences you had from childhood to adulthood. They all either strengthened or loosened ties to your beliefs. You have to understand your money story and your money beliefs in order to make any lasting changes with your finances. It is time to clean out the closet of emotions and thoughts you may have been burying deep inside of you. Acknowledge your feelings and how they may be creating a limiting mindset for you today.

Take Action

- If and when you find yourself financially triggered, listen to the part of you that is trying to be heard. What is it trying to say or warn you of? Validate those feelings and understand they may be coming from a place you are no longer in. They are trying to protect you. Acknowledge that although our feelings are a part of us, they do not need to govern what we do with money.

- Write a money autobiography. Write the story of you and money throughout your life. Pinpoint any major events that had a lasting impact on you, whether it was an experience of lack or a specific way the adults in your life managed money around you. This will help you become aware of your pain points and strengths. If you want to take this a step further, write down all the healthy coping skills that help you feel better or complete the stress cycle.

Here are a few healthy coping mechanisms you can add to your list: Talk to a trusted person, cry, exercise, meditate, laugh, do a deep breathing exercise, do something creative, take a shower.

Step 2: Get financially naked.

It is time to look at your numbers. As we discussed in chapter 4, you have to know where you are starting from to understand where you are trying to go. No more avoiding your money, overworking to compensate for your spending, or feeling like you have to live super frugally in order to get ahead. When you know your numbers, you can decide what you need to do or if you need to do anything at all.

Take Action

- Make a list of all your income, expenses, and savings. List all your checking, savings, and retirement accounts. Make sure to include where they are housed and how much money is in each of them.

- List out all your debts. Yes, all of them. Be sure to include interest rates, the total amounts owed, and your minimum monthly payments.

You can do this however you'd like: in a budget planner, on paper, with an app, in Excel—you name it. If you find yourself struggling to take this step, remember to breathe through it and give yourself some grace. If you need a little help getting started, feel free to download my free guide to getting financially naked on my website (ajaevanscounseling.com).

Step 3: Define your goals.

Once you know your numbers, it's time to define your goals. What do you want to accomplish with your money, both short-term and long-term? Think as big as you'd like. Would you like to pay off debt, pay for your child's education, go on a trip of a lifetime, retire early? The sky's the limit, so treat it as such. I know it is easy for fear and doubt to creep in, but this is not the time to limit your desires. You may not know exactly how you are going to accomplish your goals yet, but this is not the time for rational thought. Dream big. There has been a variety of research that states simply writing down your goals increases the likelihood that you will accomplish them.[52]

Please be mindful that these goals are for you. Of course, they may involve your family, friends, and other people, but these goals specifically represent how *you* want to live your best life. What do you want and need to live the life you love? Plan your goals accordingly.

Take Action

- Give yourself some time to sit and simply be. Let your imagination run free and list all the things you would like to accomplish. They don't have to be financially focused yet, just write what comes to mind. It can be in a paragraph form or a list, but get it down. Once you have your list, then you can start attaching a financial goal to each one.

Step 4: Invest in your financial education.

As you now know, financial education is not the end-all be-all, and it's important that your learning is accompanied by an attunement to your needs and personal money story. This has been proven over and over again as people struggle to stick to their budget, overspend, hoard their money, or feel like they need to compete with other people to validate themselves. The majority of what we do with our money has nothing to do with what we know about money. Financial education doesn't make you emotionally stable, and emotional stability doesn't make you good with money, so you have to have both. No matter where you stand financially, being knowledgeable about the basics allows you to make informed money decisions.

Take Action

- Go back to the financial goals you created in step 3 and highlight where your gaps in knowledge are. What financial principles do you need to learn to accomplish your goals? Do you understand them and know how to use them? If not, it's time to dive in and learn. This book has introduced you to the basics, but I encourage you to review the resources in the endnotes of this book to deepen your knowledge. Educated money moves are the best money moves!

Step 5: Create your own money plan.

Now that you know how your life experiences inform your relationship with money and you're aware of where you stand financially and what your goals are, you are prepared to put a plan together. Now, some people may want a financial professional (more on this in a bit) to help them put together an official plan, but if you feel comfortable doing this on your own, I encourage you to take that first step.

Take Action

- In reviewing your goals, separate them into two lists— short-term and long-term—then list them in order of priority. Voilà! You have a plan. I know we all want to believe money is far more complicated than it is. J. L. Collins said it perfectly when he described money as "simple not easy" in his smash hit *The Simple Path to Wealth* (the proverbial bible for those on the "financially independent retire early" journey). Committing yourself to your goals, being disciplined, and saying no when you want to say yes is hard as hell, but necessary.

Everyone is going to have a different set of priorities, but I am going to say there are a few things that should be closer to the top of your list. If you don't have one yet, an emergency fund needs to be a top priority. Yes, even before you think about paying off debt. Sometimes you can save at the same time as you pay things down, but my vote is that you build up some savings just in case something unexpected comes up. It doesn't have to be the full three to six months others advise, but you should have something set aside. Then you can work the other steps in your plan.

Step 6: Get support.

When you commit to financial wellness, it tends to impact other parts of your life. Anything we do in one part of our lives will always impact other parts. I know, I know, we are desperate to pretend we can stuff parts of ourselves down, but it so rarely works out that way. It may feel completely unrelated, but every part of who we are is connected. A holistic approach is the only real approach that provides realistic, lasting changes.

I say this because this journey can and most likely will be hard and sometimes even lonely. You may want to start having more conversations about money, and not everyone will be thrilled about it. Not to mention the social impact of potentially needing to say no to things you once did without a blink of an eye.

To combat these potential challenges, support is imperative. You are not only breaking the money taboo by talking about it but also ending shame and bringing another part of you out into the open to be free and seen. Building a supportive community around you that will help you stick to your financial boundaries will make it all a lot easier. So, start testing the waters with your friends and family and see who might be there to champion your cause.

Take Action

If you feel like you need a little bit more in-depth guidance from a professional, here are a few places to start:

- A therapist, or specifically a financial therapist, can help you sort through the emotions that come up as you work to make these money shifts.
- A financial coach can hold you accountable, assist you in creating goals, and help you smash them.
- A certified financial planner can help you build a detailed plan of action with your money for the present and future.

- A certified financial advisor can help you execute your plan so you can accomplish your goals.

I've Enjoyed Our Time Together

There you have it. When you picked up this book, you may not have been as in touch with what went into your relationship with money. There is no doubt you are now more aware of some your deep-seated thoughts and feelings about money and where you stand financially. You are not alone; all of us need this! Realizing you want to make a change and beginning the process of doing this work is the first step. While taking that first step is important, you will continuously need to make a deep dive into the history, narratives, and reality of your money experiences, especially as your life shifts. You cannot change patterns you don't know exist. But now that you have a strong foundation, you can begin to build on what you've learned here and create a new financial paradigm that benefits you now and in the future.

One of the founding pillars of my work is centered around the importance of learning and becoming our most authentic selves. It took me some time to realize why I was so passionate about this work. At the end of the day, I don't want people to feel bad about themselves. I want people to feel empowered by the strength it takes to dive into their deepest, most vulnerable parts of themselves, to come out of that journey with pride and confidence about who they truly are. Watching the results of my clients has been an honor, and I want that for you, too. But growing into your most authentic self is extremely difficult. Sometimes you don't know where to start to find out who you want to be or how you will find the courage to shift your life enough for that person to exist, but I promise it is possible. It will take courage to walk away from that job, relationship, or family dynamic, but realizing what you want and need is up to you. You have to dare to dream that you can get to that place, and it is messy. You will need to be vulnerable to do this work. It is okay to feel, to be, and to express yourself. In fact, for many of us, that is an act of rebellion in and of itself.

We all want to be seen as our most authentic selves, to be loved as that person, and to be in community with others who are accepting of us. Throughout the book, we have walked through how money can bring us closer or further away from those core ideals. And now it is up to you to decide where you want to stand moving forward. Will you step into your truth and authenticity? Will you reclaim your financial power and devote yourself to a new way of living and being? Will you allow the what-ifs and the judgments of others to keep you trapped in a shell of yourself? We all deserve to live a life of health and wealth. I believe getting your money right not only helps improve your mental health but also invites you to lead the life you want to live. Money can help or hinder, and I want it to specifically help you.

Whether your goal is financial stability for yourself and your family, generational wealth, more vacations, or improving the world by supporting organizations you believe in, it is my hope that you begin to cope appropriately with money, use it to build a beautiful life, and pour it into the things that are meaningful to you. I hope you not only enjoy it but use it to build. Use it to make the necessary changes you want to see in your life, family, community, and beyond to impact the real change.

Acknowledgments

Oh boy, where to start? So many people in my life helped me during this process. Thank you to each and every one of you who supported me while I turned this dream into a reality. No amount of words could ever truly encompass the gratitude I have for all those involved.

To my husband, I am in awe of you. When you said you were happy to be my vice president, you weren't kidding. Truly, none of this would be possible without your love, support, and willingness to always show up for our family. You gladly hopped on the emotional roller coaster that was writing a book and, outside of begrudgingly letting me type away next to you in bed, were always there to cheer me on. Thank you! Evan, Pierce, Linguini, Shelly, and I are so in love with you and are beyond lucky to have you. Thank you for always helping me shine my light brighter.

Evan and Pierce, can you believe Mommy wrote a book while you were toddlers? I can't, but I hope it makes you proud and serves as a reminder that you can do anything! I will always believe in you. Always.

Special shout out to Mom and Quinn—thank you for your unwavering belief that not only I, but we, could always accomplish anything we wanted. That foundation is the drive behind everything I do; it allowed me to believe this book could even happen.

To my friends, personal and professional, you are all a gift to my life. Between texts, calls, DMs, and celebrations, you are real ones. Thank you for supporting me, for believing in me, for pouring in when I felt like I couldn't see the light at the end of the tunnel. You consistently held space for my worries with support and wine; thank you so much.

To my book coach, Kim, I am not exaggerating when I say this book would never have been written if it wasn't for you. I will never forget your casual comment that started us on this journey—thank you. I am so grateful for the evolution of our work together and how far it has taken us. Your belief, understanding, and unbounded commitment to my voice and this project were cosmic magic. Forever tea partners and all things dangerous women, same place, same time.

To my clients, past and present, thank you for trusting me with the most vulnerable parts of your story. It is one of my greatest honors to walk beside you in your journey. You have helped me just as much as I can hope to have helped you.

To Alyn and Lyric, thank you for believing in my book and for advocating for it. Your editing prowess made this book better!

To Snehal, I am eternally grateful for you and our work. You have helped me understand myself, my needs, and my power in ways I could never have dreamed of. Thank you for making sense of my feelings when I have struggled and for grounding me when I felt unsure.

Thank you, Jenny, for helping *Feel-Good Finance* shine bright like a diamond. I can't wait for what this collaboration has in store!

To the Financial Therapy Association, thank you for building a foundation for me to do this work.

Thank you to Lindsay, Leah, Rachel, Sarah, and the whole BenBella team! Thank you for taking care of my book baby, for ushering me through the process, for editing, marketing, cover design and bringing this project forward to the world. I am so grateful.

Lastly, thank you to Grammie Travis, who nonchalantly mentioned to her granddaughter's best friend, "You should be a therapist" nearly twenty-five years ago. Your words forever changed my life.

Endnotes

1   C. DeNavas and B. D. Proctor, *Income and Poverty in the United States: 2014*, U.S. Census Bureau, September 16, 2015, https://www.census.gov/library /publications/2015/demo/p60-252.html.

2   Jonathan Shedler, "Psychodynamic Psychotherapy Brings Lasting Benefits Through Self-Knowledge," American Psychological Association, 2010, https://www.apa.org/news/press/releases/2010/01/psychodynamic-therapy.

3   Andrew C. Chang, Lisa J. Dettling, Joanne W. Hsu, and Julia Hewitt, "Disparities in Wealth by Race and Ethnicity in the 2019 Survey of Consumer Finances," FEDS Notes, Board of Governors of the Federal Reserve System, September 28, 2020, doi: 10.17016/2380-7172.2797.

4   Liz Mineo, "Racial Wealth Gap May Be a Key to Other Inequities," *Harvard Gazette*, June 3, 2021, https://news.harvard.edu/gazette/story/2021/06/racial -wealth-gap-may-be-a-key-to-other-inequities.

5   Rakesh Kochhar, "The Enduring Grip of the Gender Pay Gap," Pew Research Center, March 1, 2023, https://www.pewresearch.org/social-trends /2023/03/01/the-enduring-grip-of-the-gender-pay-gap.

6   Jeff Neumann and Tracy Matsue Loeffelholz, "40 Acres and a Mule Would Be at Least $6.4 Trillion Today—What the U.S. Really Owes Black America," *YES! Magazine*, May 14, 2015, https://www.yesmagazine.org/issue /make-right/2015/05/14/infographic-40-acres-and-a-mule-would-be-at -least-64-trillion-today.

7   Nagy A. Youssef, Laura Lockwood, Shaoyong Su, Guang Hao, and Bart P. F. Rutten, "The Effects of Trauma, with or without PTSD, on the Transgenerational DNA Methylation Alterations in Human Offsprings" *Brain Science* 8, no. 5 (May 2018): 83, doi: 10.3390/brainsci8050083.

8   David Whitebread and Sue Bingham, "Habit Formation and Learning in Young Children." Money Advice Service, May 2013, https://kidwealth.com/wp-content/uploads/the-money-advice-service-habit-formation-and-learning-in-young-children-may2013.pdf.

9   Kate Sortino, "Review of How Growing Up Low Income Messed Me Up as an Adult and How I Overcame It," Financial Diet, July 21, 2021, https://www.youtube.com/watch?v=mdQ_bxJvmu8.

10   Matthew Killingsworth, Daniel Kahneman, and Barbara Mellers, "Income and Emotional Well-Being: A Conflict Resolved," *PNAS* 120, no. 10 (March 2023): 3, doi: 10.1073/pnas.2208661120.

11   *White Hot: The Rise & Fall of Abercrombie & Fitch*, directed by Alison Klayman (Netflix, April 19, 2022).

12   Danielle Prescod, *Token Black Girl* (Seattle: Little a, 2022), 5.

13   Paul Taylor, Jeffrey Passel, Richard Fry, Richard Morin Wendy Wang, and Gabriel Velasco, "The Return of the Multi-Generational Family Household." Pew Research Center, 2010. https://www.pewresearch.org/wp-content/uploads/sites/3/2010/10/752-multi-generational-families.pdf.

14   *Trauma + The Body*, Trauma of Money, Cohort 8, 2019, https://www.thetraumaofmoney.com/.

15   Brad Klontz and Ted Klontz, *Mind Over Money: Overcoming the Money Disorders that Threaten Our Financial Health* (New York: Broadway Books, 2009).

16   "Loneliness and Social Isolation Linked to Serious Health Conditions," US Centers for Disease Control and Prevention, updated April 29, 2021, https://www.cdc.gov/aging/publications/features/lonely-older-adults.html.

17   James Grubman, *Strangers in Paradise: How Families Adapt to Wealth Across Generations* (FamilyWealth Consulting, 2013).

18   Grubman, *Strangers in Paradise*.

19   Stefanie O'Connel Rodriguez and Tiffany Aliche, "I'm tired of being 'bad with money'. Where do I even start to get my finances on track?," March 1, 2021 in *Money Confidential*. MP3 audio, 14:17, https://podcasts.apple.com/us/podcast/money-confidential/id1552942976.

20   Kristy L. Archuleta, Bradley T. Klontz, and Sonya L. Britt, eds., *Financial Therapy: Theory, Research, and Practice* (New York: Springer International Publishing, 2016).

21   Suzanne McGee and Heidi Moore, "Women's Rights and Their Money: A
      Timeline from Cleopatra to Lilly Ledbetter," *Guardian*, August 11, 2014,
      https://www.theguardian.com/money/us-money-blog/2014/aug/11/women
      -rights-money-timeline-history.

22   "The Wage Gap Among LGBTQ+ Workers in the United States," Human
      Rights Campaign, accessed August 7, 2023, https://www.hrc.org/resources
      /the-wage-gap-among-lgbtq-workers-in-the-united-states.

23   Tiffany Aliche and Mandi Woodruff-Santos, "Brown Ambition," March 2,
      2022, in Embracing the Struggle with The Broke Black Girl Dasha Kennedy,
      MP3 audio, https://www.youtube.com/watch?v=8DpiM6R32QY.

24   Aliche, Woodruff-Santos, *Brown Ambition*.

25   Lela Nargi, "Divorce Can Wreck a Woman's Financial Future. Here's How to
      Rebuild," *New York Times*, May 17, 2023, https://www.nytimes.com/2023/05
      /13/business/divorce-retirement-savings-planning.html.

26   "The Emergence of the Female Advantage in Life Expectancy," National
      Bureau of Economic Research, accessed August 8, 2023, https://www.nber
      .org/bah/2018no3/emergence-female-advantage-life-expectancy.

27   "Ellevest CEO on gaps in gender pay and investing: 'Nothing bad happens
      when women have more money,'" n.d., CNBC. Accessed May 21, 2024.
      https://www.cnbc.com/video/2020/03/06/ellevest
      -ceo-nothing-bad-happens-when-women-have-more-money.html#:~:text
      =Ellevest%20CEO%20on%20gaps%20in.

28   Linda Babcock and Sara Laschever, "The Costs of Not Negotiating,"
      Harvard Business Review, January 29, 2009, https://hbr.org/2009/01/is-talent
      -going-to-waste-in-yo.

29   Berna Anat and Erin Lowry, "Money Matters: Fireside Chat with Berna
      Anat & Erin Lowry," Author's Guild, July 28, 2023, https://authorsguild.org
      /resource/money-matters-fireside-chat-berna-anat-erin-lowry/.

30   Lisette Smith, "Move Over, Men. Here Are 4 Reasons Why Women Make
      Better Investors," The Advisory Group of San Francisco, March 20, 2023,
      https://advisorygroupsf.com/why-women-make-better-investors/.

31   Kevin Jiang, "Zeroing In on Dopamine," News and Research, Harvard
      Medical School, February 1, 2018, https://hms.harvard.edu/news/zeroing
      -dopamine.

32   K. C. Berridge, "The Debate over Dopamine's Role in Reward: The Case for
      Incentive Salience," *Psychopharmacology* 191, no. 3 (October 2006): 391–431,
      doi: 10.1007/s00213-006-0578-x.

33   *Trauma + The Body*, Trauma of Money, Cohort 8, 2019, https://www
      .thetraumaofmoney.com/.

34   "Stress Effects on the Body," American Psychological Association, updated March 8, 2023, https://www.apa.org/topics/stress/body.

35   Student Learning Programs Team, "Stress Cycles: What They Are and How to Manage Them," Stanford Teaching Commons, September 7, 2021, https://teachingcommons.stanford.edu/news/stress-cycles-what-they-are-and-how-manage-them.

36   Lauren Schwahn and Elizabeth Ayoola, "What Is the 'Cash Stuffing' Envelope System?," NerdWallet, updated October 11, 2023, https://www.nerdwallet.com/article/finance/envelope-system.

37   Susan Linney, "What Is HALT? The Dangers of Being Hungry, Angry, Lonely or Tired," American Addiction Centers, updated January 5, 2024, https://americanaddictioncenters.org/blog/common-stressors-recovery.

38   William Safire, "On Language: Up the Down Ladder," *The New York Times*, November 15, 1998. Retrieved September 20, 2023.

39   Jennifer Herrity, "Average Salary in the US (With Demographic Data)," Indeed, updated April 8, 2024, https://www.indeed.com/career-advice/pay-salary/average-salary-in-us.

40   Saprina Danise (@moneywithsaprina), TikTok video, April 28, 2023.

41   "Household Debt and Credit Report (Q4 2023)," Federal Reserve Bank of New York, accessed May 25, 2023, https://www.newyorkfed.org/microeconomics/hhdc.

42   Ali and Josh Lupo (@theficouple), Instagram post, April 29, 2023.

43   Elizabeth Scott, "Hedonic Adaptation: Why You Are Not Happier," Verywell Mind, updated June 23, 2022, https://www.verywellmind.com/hedonic-adaptation-4156926.

44   "Stress in America 2022: Concerned for the Future, Beset by Inflation," Press Releases, American Psychological Association, October 2022, https://www.apa.org/news/press/releases/stress/2022/concerned-future-inflation.

45   Jorge Sabat and Emily Gallagher, "Rules of Thumb in Household Savings Decisions: Estimation Using Threshold Regression," SSRN, September 17, 2019, doi: 10.2139/ssrn.3455696.

46   Anthony C. Klotz and Mark C. Bolino, "When Quiet Quitting Is Worse Than the Real Thing," *Harvard Business Review*, September 15, 2022, https://hbr.org/2022/09/when-quiet-quitting-is-worse-than-the-real-thing.

47   Alina Dizik, "Why You Shouldn't Ask People What They Do," BBC, August 10, 2016, https://www.bbc.com/worklife/article/20160809-why-you-shouldnt-ask-people-what-they-do.

48   Morgan Housel, *The Psychology of Money: Timeless Lessons on Wealth, Greed, and Happiness* (Hampshire, Great Britian: Harriman House, 2020), 93.

49   Dizik, "Why You Shouldn't Ask People What They Do."

50   "New Surgeon General Advisory Raises Alarm about the Devastating Impact of the Epidemic of Loneliness and Isolation in the United States," News, US Department of Health and Human Services, May 3, 2023, https:// www.hhs.gov/about/news/2023/05/03/new-surgeon-general-advisory-raises -alarm-about-devastating-impact-epidemic-loneliness-isolation-united -states.html.

51   Cory Woodroof, "Coco Gauff Thanked Her Haters after She Won the U.S. Open," For the Win, *USA Today*, September 9, 2023. https://ftw.usatoday. com/lists/coco-gauff -thanked-her-haters-us-open-win-tennis.

52   T. Epton, S. Currie, and C. J. Armitage, "Unique Effects of Setting Goals on Behavior Change: Systematic Review and Meta-analysis," *Journal of Consulting and Clinical Psychology* 85, no. 12 (December 2017): 1182–1198, doi: 10.1037/ccp0000260.

About the Author

Aja is a New York City-based licensed Mental Health Counselor specializing in Financial Therapy. With over a decade of experience, Aja has made it her mission to get louder about breaking the taboo of talking about money. Whether through writing, speaking, or consulting, Aja strives to help people better understand themselves and their relationship with money. Outside of her professional life, you can find Aja running after her two young kids in search of the next delicious place to eat.